ALEX RODRIGUEZ

ALBERT PUJOLS

RICHARD J. BRENNER

EAST END PUBLISHING, LTD.
Miller Place, New York

AUTHOR'S NOTE: Alex Rodriguez and Albert Pujols are gifted athletes, but they both had to work hard and overcome many obstacles before they were able to achieve their dreams. And, even now, they keep working on their games, trying to become the best players that they can be.

"Every time I've been down I've gotten back up by working hard every day and preparing myself to meet my goals," said Alex Rodriguez. "To me, giving my best effort is more important than achieving specific results."

You can achieve your dreams, too, if you believe in yourself and work as hard to achieve your goals as Rodriguez and Pujols work to achieve theirs. And there are lots of areas for you to consider besides athletics. You might want to become an artist or a musician or a writer; or you might decide to work for world peace or to help clean the environment. The real lesson to be learned is that you can accomplish whatever you put your mind to, as long as you're willing to work hard to achieve it.

This book is dedicated, as all my books are, to the children of the world. I wish that all of you could live in peaceful, loving surroundings, free from fear and bigotry of every type.

savedarfur.org

I want to express great appreciation to everybody whose time and talents have contributed to this book, including John Douglas, Jim Wasserman, Janie DeVos, John Backus, Bob Christopher, Jamie Calsyn, Ellen Raimondo Shupp and Rob Tringali.

I also want to express sincere thanks to Ed Masessa and Janet Speakman for their continued support.

Copy Editor: John Douglas   Book Design: Studio 31, Inc.

Photo Credits: SportsChrome supplied the following images, all of which were photographed by Rob Tringali: P. 66, 67 and 75. **Icon SMI** supplied all of the remaining photographs, as per the following, with the photographers' names in parenthesis: The cover image of **Alex Rodriguez** and the image on P. 72 (Rick Kane); P. 65 (**John Cordes**); P. 68 (**Jeff Zelevansky**); P. 69, P. 70 and P. 71 (**Anthony Causi**); The cover photo of **Albert Pujols** and the image on P. 80 (**Palm Beach Post**); P. 73 and P. 78 (**Ed Wolfstein**); P. 74 (**Peter Newcomb**); P. 76 and P. 77 (**Daniel Gluskoter**); P. 79 (**Mark Goldman**).

ISBN-10: 0-943403-74-X / ISBN-13: 978-0-943403-74-8

Published by EAST END PUBLISHING, LTD.
18 Harbor Beach Road
Miller PL, NY 11764

Printed in the United States of America by R.R. Donnelley

Richard J. Brenner, America's best-selling sportswriter, has written more than 80 exciting sports titles. For details on how to order some of them, see the back page of this book.
***
Mr. Brenner is also available to speak at schools and other venues. For details, including fees, you may e-mail him directly at: rjbrenner1@gmail.com, or write to him c/o EEP, 18 Harbor Beach Road Miller PL, NY 11764.

AUTHOR'S MESSAGE: For many years, Native American groups have been appealing to sports teams not to use names and logos that many Native American people find offensive, such as "Redskins." Out of respect for, and in support of those appeals, I have chosen not to use such names in this book. I urge all readers who agree with this position to write to the owners of the Atlanta and Cleveland teams, and to Bud Selig, the commissioner of Major League Baseball, and add your voice to those who are protesting the use of those names and logos.

TABLE OF CONTENTS

1 LIKE A SAD MOVIE

Alexander Emmanuel Rodriguez was born on July 27, 1975, becoming the third and final child of Victor and Lourdes. The birth took place in Washington Heights, which is a culturally diverse neighborhood that is located in the northern part of Manhattan. The area has long offered a landing pad for successive waves of various immigrant groups from around the world, who have come to the United States in search of increased economic opportunities and political freedom for themselves and their families.

Rodriguez's parents had come to New York from the Dominican Republic, a country located in the Caribbean, and they settled in Washington Heights because it was, and still is, home to such a large contingent of Dominicans that the neighborhood is often referred to as Little Dominica.

Although the great majority of immigrants who have come to the United States from the DR do so to escape the wide-spread poverty that continues to plague the country, that was not the case with the Rodriguezes. Lourdes and Victor, an accountant by training, had come to the U.S. not because they were desperate, but because they believed, not unreasonably, that they would be more likely to prosper in a wealthier country than in a poorer one.

After they arrived in New York, Victor bought a retail shoe store, and he worked long hours trying to build up his business. He succeeded so well in turning the store into a thriving concern that in 1979, when Alex was 4 years old, Victor was able to sell the store and move back to the DR with his family. At the time, Victor had thought that the move back home would be a permanent one but, ultimately, circumstances would arise that would undermine that expectation.

Looking back, Rodriguez remembers those childhood years spent in the DR as among the happiest in his life. He was free to run and play, and he got to spend a great deal of time with his extended family, including a large contingent of cousins, aunts, uncles and grandparents. Best of all, though, was the opportunity to spend lots of time with his father, who became his first baseball tutor. Victor, who had been a first baseman and catcher in a Dominican pro league as a young man, was an ideal teacher.

"He was the one who taught me how to play baseball," recalled Rodriguez, who first started to play the game when he was six years old. "He also spoiled me, because I was the youngest, the baby in the family. Back then, I always wanted to be like my dad."

Although Rodriguez looks back at those days as idyllic, he also remembers how challenging it was to play on the less-than-ideal fields and how children less fortunate than him had to make do with makeshift equipment.

"In the DR, playing ball was tougher than in the States, no question," said Rodriguez. "Most of the players didn't have any real equipment. In the U.S., kids have $200 gloves and play on fields that are like paradise. But in the DR, the fields are filled with rocks, and some kids play with cutout milk cartons for mitts, because they can't afford baseball gloves."

Despite the shortcomings of the fields, Rodriguez loved playing baseball, and he played it so well that he was able to compete against nine and ten year old children when he was only six.

"He was very focused from the time he was a young child, and he wasn't interested in anything else back then, just baseball," recalled his mother. "He didn't care if it was sunny or raining, he just had to play ball. If I didn't take him to the park every day, he would cry."

In 1983, four years after they had moved to the DR, the family moved back to the United States because economic reversals had forced Victor to go back into business. This time, they settled in Kendall, Florida, a suburb of Miami, which sits on the edge of the Florida Everglades. Although Rodriguez had loved living with all his relatives in the DR, he knew that his parents were doing what they thought was best for the family, and he adapted to the move without complaint.

"Sometimes, parents get kicked down by life," explained Rodriguez, referring to his father's need to rebuild the family's financial structure. "It happened to my parents when I was eight. They told me that we'd move back to the Dominican in a few months, but we never did. It didn't upset me; I just took it in stride."

Victor opened another shoe store, this time in Miami, but after a year in Florida, he decided that he wanted to move back to New York City. His wife, however, didn't want to have to pick-up and move again, and she thought that it would be better for the children if they were allowed to stay put and establish roots where they were.

After realizing that he wasn't going to be able to convince Lourdes to change her mind, Victor left for New York by himself, leaving their home without even saying good-bye to Alex, who, at the time, was nine years old. One day, he was there, a hard-working, loving father, who was teaching his son how to play baseball, and the next day he was gone, without a word of explanation. It would, in fact, be many years before Victor even called and spoke to his son on the telephone.

"I didn't know what was going on," recalled Rodriguez, who has never really recovered from that sense of being abandoned by his father. "I thought he was coming back. I thought he had just gone to the store, or something, and that he would be coming back."

Lourdes had told her two older children that their father's leaving was permanent, but she didn't have the heart to share that news with her youngest child. For months, Rodriguez went on believing that his father might walk in the family's front door at any moment, and that his life would go back to being the way it had always been, the way that he had wanted it to stay.

"But he never did come back," said Rodriguez, the hurt playing in his eyes like a sad movie. "I kept thinking that my father would come back, but he never did."

When Victor walked away from his family, he not only created an emotional hole in his son's sense of well-being, he also left them in a serious financial bind. Suddenly cast as the family's breadwinner, Lourdes had to take on two jobs to support herself and her three children. During the day, she worked in an office, as a secretary, and at night, she waited tables in a restaurant, hoping that the tips she made would help her to clothe and feed her children and also cover the family's other monthly expenses.

"It was definitely hard," said Rodriguez, the crack in his voice reinforcing his words. "I did my best to help out by doing household chores and bringing home good grades, because I knew that would make my mother proud."

On most nights, when she came home, her youngest son would be there, waiting to tally her tips.

"I used to sit at the kitchen table and count the coins and bills from the tips that my mother brought home," recalled Rodriguez. "Fifty dollars was a good night."

"I consider my mom to be my MVP, Most Valuable Parent," he continued, smiling at his own quip. "All the love I had for my father, I just gave it all to my mother. She deserved it. She's one of my best friends."

2   ENJOY THE SWEAT

Although his father's desertion had left a hole in his heart, Rodriguez did, at least, inherit Victor's athletic genes, and he was fortunate to wind up in Florida, where he could, if he chose, play baseball year-round. But what was given could never really make up for what had been taken away.

"I tried to tell myself that it didn't matter, but I was just lying to myself," acknowledged Rodriguez. "When I was alone, I often cried, and wondered where my father was. To this day, I don't really know how a man could do that—turn his back on his family."

The absence of Victor, who had slipped so silently out of his family's life, has sent Rodriguez on a life-long quest in search of men who could provide the kindness and guidance that his father's absence had deprived him of. And while he has, largely, been fortunate to meet a few such men, none of them have filled the void created by his father's desertion.

"I feel as though I've always had good male leadership and mentorship around me," said Rodriguez. "I try not to focus on what's missing; I prefer to look at the glass as half full."

The first and, perhaps, the most important of those mentors was Eddie Rodriguez, a former minor league player, who is the director of the Hank Kline Boys and Girls Club in Miami. To this day, Alex still considers

Rodriguez, who is not related to him, to be the most important influence in his life.

"Definitely," said Alex, in an interview conducted a couple of years ago. "Off the field, it's Eddie Rodriguez. I've been at the Boys and Girls Club since I was 8 years old. Now, I'm 29, and 21 years later, he's still hitting me ground balls. He's been a good mentor and friend."

The ties that bind the two together are so strong that Alex has donated more than two million dollars to the Club, and sometimes still uses its facilities for his off-season workouts.

The first time Eddie Rodriguez saw Alex handle himself on the baseball diamond, he knew that he was seeing someone who had great talent, and Rodriguez was a good judge of baseball talent, having coached a number of boys who went on to big league fame, including Rafael Palmeiro, only the fourth player in major league history to collect 500 home runs and 3,000 hits in a career, and Jose Canseco, the first player ever to hit 40 big flies and steal 40 bases in the same season.

"Alex was special," recalled Rodriguez. "I don't mean that I knew he was going to be a major leaguer the first time I saw him. You never know that when they're eight years old. All you could tell then was that he had talent, and that he was never afraid to work hard and do things the right way.

"We've had a lot of players come through the club, but nobody who has ever come through our doors ever worked harder than Alex."

Another important father figure to Rodriguez was Juan Arteaga, who was the father of J.D., a boy who would become Rodriguez's best friend. The senior

Arteaga coached teams that the boys played on, and he also wound up treating Rodriguez as if he was a second son.

The relationship between Alex and the Arteagas began one day while Rodriguez was watching J.D. and his team practice baseball on a neighborhood field. Juan Arteaga, the team's coach, noticed the young boy staring intently at the other boys, looking like a hungry kid salivating over a stack of food that's just beyond his reach. Touched by what he saw, Arteaga invited Rodriguez to join the practice and, even though he was a year or two younger than the other players, he immediately showed that he could play with the best of them.

The two boys, who lived a few streets away from one another, quickly became the best of friends, while Juan Arteaga became Rodriguez's coach and stand-in father. When he and his son would go to a baseball game, Rodriguez was asked to join them and, when Rodriguez needed equipment that his mother couldn't afford, Juan Arteaga would step up and buy it for him.

"Mr. Arteaga and Eddie Rodriguez guided me and gave me their most precious gift—time," recalled Alex. "I made sure that I didn't do anything stupid that would let them down."

A short while after Arteaga began coaching Rodriguez he told J.D. something that startled his son—that Rodriguez was the best player he had ever seen.

"Alex was only 11, and I thought my dad was crazy," recalled J.D. "How could he think that an 11-year-old kid was the best player he had ever seen? But now, I have to say that my father was a pretty good scout."

In addition to finding suitable father figures in his everyday life, Rodriguez proved that he was also a good judge of athletic role models, always choosing players who weren't merely superstars, but who also demonstrated a willingness to work hard, exhibit good sportsmanship, and be outstanding members of their communities.

"My mom always said, 'I don't care if you turn out to be a terrible player, I just want you to be a good person,'" explained Rodriguez. "That's the most important thing to me. Like Cal Ripken or Dale Murphy, I want people to look at me and say, 'He's a good person.'"

Murphy, who was a center fielder for Atlanta, and Cal Ripken Jr., the Iron Man shortstop for the Baltimore Orioles, who played in a record-setting 2,632 consecutive games, were, along with Keith Hernandez, who was a clutch-hitting, slick fielding first baseman for the New York Mets, Rodriguez's favorite baseball players.

"Cal Ripken was the only shortstop I knew of who hit third in the lineup, the spot where most teams put their best hitter," said Rodriguez, whose favorite position was shortstop. "And he was also a Gold Glove fielder. That's the type of player that I wanted to be."

Like most boys his age, Rodriguez was also a big fan of Michael Jordan, who was the high-flying basketball superstar of the Chicago Bulls, but he admired *His Airness* more for his outstanding work ethic than for his sheer talent.

"I've always enjoyed practice more than playing games," explained Alex. "Practice, to me, is where you hone your craft. I have a great passion for constantly trying to improve.

"I live by the idea that you have to enjoy your sweat, because while hard work doesn't guarantee success, without it, you don't have a chance."

When Rodriguez talks about working hard, he isn't merely paying lip service to the concept, as every coach he has ever played for has discovered.

"While the other boys would be sleeping, I'd find Alex doing crunches and sit-ups at seven in the morning," recalled Tony Quesada, one of the coaches on a traveling team that Rodriguez played for when he was in junior high school. "Even then, you would see that he had that special spark, the inner drive to perfect his skills."

After night games, Rodriguez would still want to practice, so he would try to enlist teammates to stay on the field with him.

"The park employees would turn out the lights after games, wanting to go home, and Alex would still want people to hit him ground balls in the dark," recalled former teammate James Colzie II. "I mean, we all wanted to do well, but Alex took it to a whole different level. We wanted it, but he was willing to do more to go get it."

Rodriguez would also arise early in the morning and get to the field by 6:30, so that he could squeeze in some extra practice before school started.

"They thought I was a lunatic," said Alex. "After three months I ran out of friends to hit to me. I finally had to stop because school officials said I was getting too sweaty and smelly before class."

Rodriguez also used to watch baseball games on television, although not like a typical fan does by rooting for a specific team. Rodriguez studied particular players, learning how to play the game by watching the way they approached different situations.

"When I arrived in the big leagues, no one had to tell me that Cal Ripken was a pull hitter, or what Darryl Strawberry did when he had two strikes on him," explained Rodriguez. "My knowledge of those players and my understanding of the game shortened my learning curve, *big-time*."

3 FACING DOWN THE PRESSURE

During the summer of 1988, when Rodriguez was 13 years old, he suddenly felt that baseball had grown as stale as a three-day-old cake. After seven years of playing countless games, from the rutted fields of the DR, to the pristine diamonds that he played on with elite travel teams, Rodriguez felt as though he had had enough of the game, and that he would rather concentrate his athletic efforts on playing basketball.

He was such an exceptional hoopster that, in the fall of 1989, he became the first freshman in two decades to make the varsity at Christopher Columbus High School. He also made the varsity baseball team the following spring, but the coach didn't give him much playing time, and told him that he shouldn't expect to become a starter until his senior season.

"I thought about focusing on basketball, instead," he recalled. "Mom called a family meeting to discuss it, and we talked about my options. She finally convinced me to give baseball one more season."

His mother also wanted him to transfer from Columbus, which is a large public school, and attend a smaller, private high school, which she felt would provide a better educational opportunity. When the Arteagas heard that news, they made a beeline to the Rodriguez home and convinced them that Alex should attend the school that J.D. was attending, Westminster Christian, a school with only 300 students, which enjoyed a reputation for having strong academic and athletic programs.

Fortunately for Rodriguez, he was a very good student, which made it possible for him to receive a partial scholarship from the school, a not unimportant fact for his mother, who had to scrimp and save to come up with the tuition payments.

"I always did my homework and prepared myself to succeed in the classroom, just like I did on the baseball diamond," explained Rodriguez, who knew that there was a lot more to get out of life than simply pounding a baseball. "I liked doing homework, because it prepared me for the classroom, just the way practicing prepared me for games."

After his successful recruiting trip to the Rodriguez home, Mr. Arteaga had paid a visit to Westminster's baseball coach, Rich Hoffman, and told him that he was about to get the best young player in the Miami area.

"People are always telling me that they've seen the next Barry Bonds, the second coming of Roger Clemens," said Hoffman, with a dismissive snort. "If the people really knew what they were talking about, I'd have a team of future Hall of Famers every season."

Although Hoffman hadn't, at that time, coached any players who were on their way to Cooperstown, he had created a powerhouse program that consistently turned out top-notch squads, including the 1990 version, which had just won the Florida state AA title, and had finished the season as the 10th ranked team in the country, according to the *USA Today* poll.

During the fall semester of Rodriguez's first year at Westminster, he was dealt a heavy blow when Juan

Arteaga, a man who had done so much to help him get where he was, suffered a heart attack and died while watching a football game at the school.

"It was a big blow to me," acknowledged Rodriguez. "Everything he gave to J.D., he gave to me. He was the father I didn't have in my life. I still play in his honor."

When Rodriguez reported for spring baseball tryouts, he discovered another sad fact: 13 of the players from the state title team were returning, and how much playing time he would receive was very much up in the air.

"Alex certainly didn't have the look of a superstar," recalled Hoffman. "He was a tall, thin, not very strong kid. But you could see by the way he moved that he was an athlete. That helped him in the field, but he wasn't anywhere close to being a finished product as a hitter."

At the start of the Warriors 1991 season, Rodriguez split time at shortstop with two other players and, when he finally did win the starting job later in the season, it was because of what he did with his glove, not because of his work with the stick.

"He swung at a lot of pitches that weren't in the same zip code as home plate," recalled Hoffman, with a chuckle. "He worked hard, but he didn't have any discipline as a hitter."

While he didn't do any significant damage to opposing pitchers throughout most of that first season with the Warriors, he did clout a two-run dinger in the district finals, which provided J.D. Arteaga, who was on the mound, with all the runs he needed. Although he had struggled at the plate and the school failed in its bid to repeat as state champion, Rodriguez knew that he had two years remaining at Westminster, and he was determined to do what he had to do to improve his hitting and help get the team back to the championship game.

During that summer, he worked out every day, added muscle to his body by lifting weights, and also grew a couple of inches. By the time he returned to school for the fall semester, he stood 6'2" and weighed in at 180 pounds of sinewy muscle. The first reward for all that work occurred that fall on the football field, when Rodriguez quarterbacked the Warriors to a 9-1 record, and earned recognition as one of the top high school players in football-mad Florida.

One of his top passing targets was the tight end, Doug Mientkiewicz, who has gone on to have a long career as a major league first baseman.

"Alex had an amazing arm, and he was so quick on his feet," said Mientkiewicz, who is anything but swift-footed. "If he had stuck with football, he probably could have played in the NFL."

Rodriguez then turned his astonishing athletic attention to basketball, and he quickly established himself as the Warriors' high-scoring point guard, where he was equally adept at running the team or threading the nets, as he did one night when he poured in 43 points.

"He definitely could have been a big-time college quarterback or point guard," declared James Colzie II, who edged out Rodriguez in the voting for the 1992-1993 Dade County Athlete of the Year award, and is now a college football coach. "He's a phenomenal athlete."

Rodriguez continued to show off his athleticism the following spring, when he scorched opposing pitchers for a .477 average and also stole 42 bases without being thrown out even once. His breakout season not only earned him a place on the 1992 prep school All-America team, it also caught the attention of college coaches and big league scouts.

Most importantly, his outstanding performance helped the Warriors post a 32-2 record, win the Florida state championship, and finish the 2002 season as the top-ranked team in the *USA Today* poll.

Although his success on the diamond could, in part, be traced to his added muscle tone, the more important factor was all the time he had spent in the backyard batting cage of Doug Mientkiewicz.

"Alex was always at my house," recalled Mientkiewicz, who would one day wind up as Rodriguez's teammate in the big leagues. "Our whole group was pretty close-knit, and my home was the flop-house. Even if I went out on a date one night, when I got home, they'd be there, taking their swings."

It was a golden period in the lives of the group, one that still shines as brightly in their minds as it did then.

"Those were great times," recalled Rodriguez, who also starred in the classroom and earned a place on Westminster's academic honor roll. "We were all 15, 16 years old, and we were playing sports all year round. We went from football to basketball to baseball. That's all a kid wants to do."

Rodriguez removed himself from the sports merry-go-round the following fall however, after he suffered an injury early in the 2002 football season. While he was on the sidelines, he decided to skip the remainder of the football season and devote all his athletic energies to baseball.

Even before the season had started, though, Rodriguez began to feel an extraordinary amount of pressure from college recruiters, who all but set up tents on the family's front lawn. And once the season started, big league scouts watched his every move, trying to accurately judge where he should be picked in the annual draft of amateur players, which was scheduled for June 3.

"I was just a kid, and scouts were talking about what I would be doing in two or three years," recalled Rodriguez, who knew that if he did well and lived up to the outsized expectations, that he could secure a college scholarship, or sign with a big league team for a great deal of money. "That's an awful lot of pressure to be under. Especially at that time, when I was so young and still learning about myself and life."

Even Hoffman, who has coached a great many all-star players, was amazed at the three-ring circus atmosphere that his teenage star had to cope with.

"You can't imagine the pressure-wringer that he had to go through," recalled Hoffman. "We had big crowds everywhere we played, and they all came to watch Alex. I've never seen a high school player command so much attention. Unlike a lot of players I've seen who couldn't handle the scrutiny, Alex thrived on it. It made him work even harder."

Rodriguez's mother tried to help her son by letting him know that there was a positive side to all the attention.

"The scouts are here because they must see things that they like," said Lourdes. "Don't change anything, just be yourself."

However, there was one element that did need altering, and Larry Corrigan, who was working as a scout for the Minnesota Twins, provided the motivation. At a time when Rodriguez's head had swollen past his hat size, Corrigan told Rodriguez that he needed to stop behaving like a spoiled superstar, and start focusing on his baseball development.

"Corrigan was one of the most influential people in my career," recalled Rodriguez, who has enough humility to be able to tell this story on himself. "When I was 17 years old, during my senior season, he pulled me aside and told me to stop being a prima donna, and that he would be watching me from that day on. I took the game a lot more seriously after hearing his message, and I was a lot more focused on details from there on."

With his priorities back in place, Rodriguez was able to deflect the constant pressure that was being applied, and went on to post a .505 average, along with nine home runs and 36 RBI in 33 games. He had come a long way in his three seasons at Westminster, progressing from being a part-time fill-in, to a full-fledged superstar, whose room overflowed with trophies and awards. But his final game with the Warriors was turned into a painful memory when Westminster suffered an excruciating late-inning loss in post-season play.

Ironically, the Warriors had looked as though they were about to move a step closer to a second consecutive state title when Rodriguez hit a go-ahead home run in the seventh inning of the regional finals. But, two innings later, he turned into the game's goat, when his third error of the day allowed the winning run to score, which ended the team's season and his high school career.

"It was probably the most crushed I've ever felt on a baseball field," said Rodriguez, who had already been selected as the top overall pick in the amateur draft. "That was my last memory before going off to professional baseball, and it humbled me so much that I thought, 'Hey, even when you think you're the very best in the country, the No. 1 pick, you can still make the biggest goofball mistake and lose the most important game of the season.'"

4   A SUMMER TO REMEMBER

Although his final game at Westminster had ended badly, his senior season had still been a crowning success. He had been selected as the USA Junior Baseball Player of the Year and the Gatorade National High School Baseball Player of the Year. He had also been the only high school player chosen as a finalist for the Golden Spikes award, which is annually given to the top amateur player in the country. The award almost always goes to a college player, as it did that year, when Darren Dreifort, a starting pitcher for Wichita State, was named the winner.

For Rodriguez, though, the awards and the recognition may have taken a back seat to the day that Cal Ripken, who was in Florida for spring training, showed up at one of his games and, afterwards, spent time talking to the star-struck shortstop.

"Our styles are pretty much alike," Ripken told reporters. "Alex has a real good chance to become the best shortstop ever."

At the time, Ripken's praise seemed a bit over the top, although it would, soon enough, prove to be acutely perceptive. For Rodriguez, however, the exact words were less important than the opportunity to meet a boyhood idol.

"I couldn't wait to run home and tell my family that Cal Ripken knew my name," Rodriguez confided. "I mean, I had a poster of him hanging in my bedroom. It was a dream come true."

It seemed that the good times couldn't get much better after the Seattle Mariners, who held the top draft pick in 1993, used the choice to select Rodriguez.

"He has all the tools," raved Roger Jongewaard, who was Seattle's scouting director. "He can run, hit for average, hit for power, field and throw."

The Mariners had debated internally about whether to choose Rodriguez, a high school shortstop, who, at best, would probably take three or four years to work his way to the majors, or Darren Dreifort, a college pitcher, who might be major league-ready in two years or less.

To help them finalize their choice, the Mariners had Rodriguez come to Seattle for a workout with the team, and he put on a display of hitting and fielding that simply dazzled everyone who was there. But, what was equally impressive to the Mariners was the level of maturity that he demonstrated with the way he spoke and carried himself.

"You don't see many guys when they're 17 years old who can walk on to a big league ball field and look like they should stay right there," recalled sportscaster Dave Valle, who was a Seattle catcher at the time. "He looked like he was born to be there. He *was* a big leaguer, and there were no two ways about it. And after he made it, he worked even harder. As a player, as a competitor and as an opponent, one of the things people respect about him most is that he shows up to play every day."

The Mariners front office was so impressed with what they had seen and how the teenager had conducted himself that they decided to invest their pick in Rodriguez, while Dreifort wound up being selected by the Los Angeles Dodgers, who picked second. The Mariners weren't alone in thinking that they had picked the amateur player with the most upside in the draft, and one of the highest-rated draftees ever.

"He's the best prospect I've ever seen," raved the scouting director of an American League team. "He might be the best player *ever* in the draft. He's as talented as Ken Griffey Jr., (who was the Mariners' All-Star center fielder) but he plays with more intensity. The Mariners loved Dreifort, but they couldn't pass on this kid."

The news of the Mariners' decision arrived while Rodriguez was in attendance at a draft-day party at the Arteaga home, and it was received with mixed feelings. Rodriguez was certainly delighted to be selected as the No. 1 overall pick, but he was definitely not thrilled at being chosen by the Mariners.

For one thing, Seattle looked like a sorry excuse for a major league franchise, with only one winning season to show for its 16 years of otherwise futile existence. For another, their home field at the time, the Kingdome, was one of the game's least attractive stadiums, and Seattle was farther away from Miami than any other city in the major leagues. If he had to play for a team that was in a different time zone, Rodriguez had hoped that it would at least be a National League franchise, so that, after he made it to the majors, his family and friends could watch him play when the team came to Miami to play the Florida Marlins.

While he was dealing with those mixed emotions, Rodriguez received another call, and heard a voice that he hadn't heard in eight years. When he placed the receiver to his ear, he was startled to hear the voice of his father, offering his congratulations.

"I didn't know what to think," said Rodriguez, who, while celebrating his exciting future, had suddenly been pulled back into his painful past. "It was awkward for both of us, and after a few minutes, he was gone again."

Despite his unhappiness at being drafted by Seattle, Rodriguez didn't have another viable choice, unless he decided to accept the offer of a scholarship from the University of Miami. But, since his heart was set on getting started with his professional career as quickly as he could, he hired the high-profile, hard-nosed sports agent Scott Boras to negotiate with the Mariners on his behalf. Negotiations with Boras often turn into long-drawn-out affairs, and this one was not going to be an exception.

While those discussions between the Mariners and Boras went forward, Rodriguez became the first high school player ever to be invited to try out for the USA National Team. But that exciting possibility turned into a negative experience, because Rodriguez, on the advice of Boras, refused to allow Topps, the team's sponsor, to create a player card for him without paying him for the use of his picture. Because of that refusal, he was cut from the team, and experienced his first taste of the business side of sports.

"If I had signed with them, it would have cost me at least $500,000 in lost income from another card company that was willing to pay me for the use of my photo," explained Rodriguez. "That was a lot of money to leave on the table."

Later in the summer, as the negotiations between Boras and the Mariners continued to drag out,

Rodriguez was selected to play for the U.S. Junior National Team, in a tournament in San Antonio, Texas, against national junior teams from other countries. He was very much looking forward to the competition, since he had had a wonderful experience when he played with the U.S. team at the 1992 World Junior Championships in Monterey, Mexico. Although he excelled in the tournament, as he led all players with six big flies, and also racked up 16 RBI in 13 games, his most lasting impressions from Monterey weren't about his statistics, but about meeting players from around the world.

"I don't recall the scores of any of the games," noted Rodriguez. "But I do remember how interesting it was to meet players from different cultures."

Rodriguez got off to a good start in San Antonio, collecting four hits in the first two games, but the experience turned suddenly negative when an errant warm-up throw struck him just below the right eye. The impact knocked him out and broke his right cheekbone and, as bad as the accident was, it just barely missed being a whole lot worse.

"If the ball had struck an inch higher, I could have been killed," said Rodriguez, who was experiencing the most momentous summer of his young life. "An inch to the side, and I might have lost an eye."

While he was at home recovering from the injury and waiting for his first professional contract to be finalized, he began a friendship with Derek Jeter, a young shortstop, who had been the New York Yankees' top draft pick a year earlier. Jeter was able to provide Rodriguez with first-hand insight about life in the minor leagues and about how to deal with the lofty expectations that come with being a high draft pick.

"Derek and I hit it off right away," recalled Rodriguez. "He was a big help, and made it easier for me to adjust to my new situation."

But the advice seemed premature because, as Labor Day approached, the contract negotiations remained stalled and the clock was ticking close to the signing deadline, which was August 31, the day on which Rodriguez would start attending classes at the University of Miami. Once he enrolled in school, the Mariners would forfeit their rights to him, and Rodriguez wouldn't be eligible to sign with another team until the June 1994 draft.

Finally, on the day before the looming deadline, a deal was struck that called for Rodriguez to receive a three-year contract that would pay him $1.3 million dollars. At the press conference called to announce the agreement, Rodriguez, who had been anxiously awaiting this moment for nearly three months, was asked what his goal was. His response was direct and to the point.

"I want to be in the big leagues as soon as possible."

5 A RISING STAR ON THE HORIZON

After the contract was signed, the Mariners flew Rodriguez to Seattle, where he spent some time hanging out with Ken Griffey, Jr., the team's reigning superstar, who had been the team's top pick in the 1987 draft. Griffey took Rodriguez out to dinner and gave him the lowdown on what life in Seattle was all about. Afterwards, they went back to Griffey's house, where they played video games, while Junior playfully ribbed Rodriguez about all the long bus rides he would be taking as he played his way up through the Mariners' minor league system.

Almost as soon as the first check from Seattle had been cashed, Rodriguez paid off the mortgage on his mother's house, bought her a new car, and gave her all the money that she needed to retire from her job.

"My mom is the whole world to me," he explained. "She deserves everything I can give her, because she's done so much for me."

Rodriguez also bought himself a Jeep, and arranged for Boras to send him a modest monthly allowance. But the remainder of the money was put to work in various investments, which were intended to help secure Rodriguez's financial future, independent of any income that he might make from baseball.

A few weeks after he signed his name on the contract, Rodriguez began his professional career with Seattle's entry in the Arizona Instructional League, where he had the opportunity to show what he could do against other major league hopefuls. After only a few games, the team's manger, John McNamara, knew that the Mariners had picked wisely, and gave Rodriguez a ringing endorsement.

"This kid is the real deal," said McNamara, who had been a big league manager for three different franchises. "He's got real soft hands, terrific range and an A+ arm. He'll have to learn how to hit major league pitching, but he'll adjust. He has as much talent as any teenager that I've ever seen."

After the finish of the league's short season, Rodriguez returned to his mother's home in Kendall, and began to prepare himself for the 1994 season. During that time in Florida, he worked out almost every day, dividing his time between the gym, where he lifted weights and ran on a treadmill, and a baseball diamond, where he fielded grounders and hit for as long as he could find people to pitch to him.

"If I wasn't going to make it, it wasn't going to be because I didn't try my hardest," said Rodriguez. "I knew that nobody was going to be impressed with what I had done in high school. I realized that I was, in a sense, starting out all over again."

The Mariners decided to give Rodriguez a small taste of big league life by having him spend a brief time with the team at their spring training site in 1994. Although his time at the camp was short, the way he handled himself created a big impression on Lou Piniella, who was Seattle's manager.

"You get vibes from young players," explained Piniella, who is now the manager of the Chicago Cubs.

"A kid who's scared, sits at the end of the bench. When I was ready to make my substitutions, Alex always became very visible. He would grab his glove or his bat, depending upon the situation. In his own way, he was telling me that he was ready, that he wasn't afraid to compete."

After his short stint with Seattle, Rodriguez was sent, as planned, to the Appleton (Wisconsin) Timber Rattlers, the franchise's Class-A team in the Midwest League. The strategy that had been mapped out by the Mariners' staff called for Alex to play half a season with the Timber Rattlers and then, if he played as well as they had hoped he would, move up to their Double-A affiliate in Jacksonville (Florida), in the Southern League.

It took all of two games with Appleton for Rodriguez to start convincing people that he was on an express train to the big leagues. In his first game, which was played against the Madison Hatters, Rodriguez caught everyone's attention when he went deep into the hole between short and third to backhand a hard grounder that had been ticketed for a single to left, then pivot around and, in one motion, make a long throw across the diamond to the first baseman that nailed the startled Hatter runner at first.

The play, which showed off Rodriguez's range, arm strength and accuracy, made an immediate and lasting impression on Joe McEwing, a Madison infielder, who was also on his way to the majors, although moving at a much slower pace than Rodriguez.

During that first game, McEwing also noticed that Rodriguez had looked terrible in two at-bats, as he watched him strike out twice while helplessly flailing away at curve balls that had made him seem overmatched. But, after the following game, McEwing realized that Rodriguez not only had great skills, but that he was also a quick read, who could make incredible strides in a very short time.

"The next night he hit a home run over the left field fence, and then lashed a double off the right-center field fence, on the same breaking balls he had looked silly on the night before," recalled McEwing, amazed at Rodriguez's ability to grow his game so quickly. "You could tell even then that he was pretty special."

Over the course of the next few weeks, Rodriguez's average hovered around the .280 mark, a solid average for almost any player, especially for a first-year player who is also dealing with his first extended time away from home. But for Rodriguez, whose average had soared off the charts when he was in high school, .280 seemed like the mark of failure. He became so discouraged and, perhaps, homesick, that he called his mother and told her that he was thinking about quitting and coming back to Florida. But Lourdes, who understood the need for courage and determination, wasn't about to indulge her son's insecurities.

"I don't want you home with that defeatist attitude," his mother had scolded. "You just go out and play hard, and everything will be fine."

Whether it was coincidental or not, Rodriguez quickly began a 16-game hitting rampage, during which he hammered 11 home runs and racked up 31 RBI, while posting a .406 average.

"You can spend a lifetime as a manager and never see a player of his caliber," said Carlos Lezcano, who was the Timber Rattlers' manager. "It wasn't only what he did with the stick, he fielded his position with the grace of a ballet dancer, and he ran the bases like a deer."

Rodriguez also impressed people with his friendly personality and down-to-earth manner, which didn't show a trace of arrogance about his contract or his press clippings.

"I don't know anyone who doesn't like Alex," said Raul Ibanez, who was one of Rodriguez's teammates at Appleton and then again in Seattle. "You knew he was a No. 1 pick and got a nice contract, and would go to the majors quick. But he was good with everyone, just one of the guys on the club."

After playing in only 65 games with Appleton, during which time he hit for a .319 average, hit 14 dingers and drove in 55 runs, Rodriguez was promoted to Jacksonville, a step that usually takes even fast-rising players a full year to make. The majority of the players at the Double-A level have usually spent at least two seasons in the minors, and most of them are in their early 20's. Rodriguez, who was only 18 years old, was unfazed by his quick promotion, and announced his arrival to the Southern League by hitting a home run in his first at-bat.

On July 7th, after only 17 games with Jacksonville, Rodriguez was told to pack his bags and fly to Boston, where Seattle was scheduled to play a three-day weekend series against the Red Sox. The following day, only 13 months after he had graduated from high school, Rodriguez made his major-league debut in Boston's fabled Fenway Park, and became the youngest player to see action in the big leagues since Jose Rijo pitched for the New York Yankees in 1984, 37 days shy of his 19th birthday.

"If it doesn't work out, I'm the one who's going to be criticized," said Lou Piniella. "I lobbied the front office to bring him up."

Piniella knew that he might be rushing Rodriguez into a situation that the teenage shortstop wasn't ready to handle after such a short stint in the minors. But, he had been unhappy with the glove work of his middle infielders, and he hoped that Rodriguez could help shore up Seattle's leaky defense.

"Let's face it, if we were in the middle of a pennant race, we would have left him at Jacksonville," acknowledged Piniella. "But we're not even playing .500 ball, and we figured he'd be ready next year, anyway. So, I'm just pushing the button a little faster than I thought I would."

Although even Rodriguez didn't know if he was prepared for the task of standing up to big league pitching, he put on a brave face for Piniella and tried to cover his own nervousness and excitement with bravado.

"Don't worry," he told Piniella, just before taking the field for his major league debut. "I'm ready for this."

Although he took an 0-for-3 collar in that first game, there wasn't a happier person in all of Beantown.

"Last year I would have paid anything to watch a major league game," said Rodriguez, only the third 18-year-old shortstop since 1900 to play in the majors. "This year I'm playing in one."

Rodriguez collected his first two big league hits in his next game against the Red Sox, and then the Mariners returned home to face the Yankees. In his first game in front of the hometown fans, Rodriguez showed Piniella the type of defense that he had been looking for when he raced to his left and flagged down an up-the-middle bouncer with a diving stab of his outstretched glove. As he tumbled to the ground, Rodriguez switched the ball to his right hand, bounced back up, and released the ball, all in one sweet, acrobatic motion. His throw thumped into the web of the first baseman's glove a moment before the speedy Bernie Williams touched the bag, drawing a standing ovation from the Seattle fans, and a smile from Piniella.

"That, gentlemen, was big league defensive," said Piniella, as reporters gathered in his office after the game. "And if anyone missed it, they can catch it on the tube, because that was a highlight play, no doubt about it."

But his fine defense couldn't cover all the holes in his swing, and after only 17 games with Seattle, Rodriguez, who was hitting .204, was optioned to the Mariners' Triple-A team in Calgary, Alberta, Canada.

"I gave it my best shot, but at 18 years old, I wasn't ready to hit against major league pitchers," said Rodriguez. "It could have been easy to get down on myself, but I wasn't going to let a disappointment derail me."

Although he hadn't been ready to hold his own against major league pitching, his remarkably rapid ascent through the Mariners' minor league system had also convinced his manager and the front office that they had a rising star on the horizon.

"He'll be back," promised Piniella. "That young man has all the tools to be an All-Star in this league for a long, long time."

6   LIFE'S HARD EDGES

In an attempt to quicken the pace of his baseball development and accelerate his return to the big leagues, Rodriguez decided to go to the Dominican Republic, a place that still evoked pleasant childhood memories, to play in the Winter League.

Instead of improving, however, Rodriguez's skills seemed to decline, and those months in the DR turned out to be the most trying of times for him.

"It was the toughest experience of my life," said Rodriguez, who hit for a .179 average during his twelve weeks of utter futility. "I kept thinking I was going to turn things around, but I never did. I just got my tail kicked and learned how hard this game can be. It was brutal, but I recommend it to every young player."

As if he didn't have enough to deal with during that dark time, his father added to his discomfort by showing up one day while Rodriguez was taking batting practice.

"When he told me who he was, I almost broke down, right on the field," recalled Rodriguez. "I told him that I would go to lunch with him the next day."

But Rodriguez, who was still filled with so much resentment toward the parent who had abandoned him, decided to cancel the appointment.

"I couldn't go and see him just like that," explained Rodriguez, who hadn't had enough time to prepare for the emotional encounter. "I wasn't ready to let go of my anger and hurt."

Despite his poor performance in Winter League play, Rodriguez had still hoped to make a strong showing at spring training and establish himself as Seattle's starting shortstop for the 1995 season. But as it turned out, he still wasn't ready to compete against big league pitching, and spent the season shuttling back and forth between Seattle and the Mariners' Triple-A team in Tacoma, Washington. Although the distance between the two cities is only 30 minutes, the trips back to Tacoma were the longest, saddest trips he had ever had to make.

"Each demotion chipped away at my confidence," recalled Rodriguez. "The last time, in mid-August, I sat at my Seattle locker with my head down, in tears. I felt drained, defeated."

He became so discouraged that, once again, he thought about quitting and enrolling at the University of Miami. In a phone call to his mother, he vented his hopes, fears and disappointments.

"I have nothing left to prove at triple-A," said Rodriguez, who tattooed Triple-A pitchers for a .354 average, racking up 15 home runs and 45 RBI in the 54 games that he played with the Rainiers. "I want to play in the majors. Maybe it would have been better if I had gone to college. Hopefully, next year I'll have *one* address."

During one of his stays with the Mariners, Rodriguez had a chance encounter that made him realize that he wasn't working as hard as he thought he was, and that he was going to have to expend more effort than he had been. The lesson was learned when he went to the King-dome to retrieve a cell phone that he had left there after taking batting practice earlier in the day. Because the team had an open date, he had expected the clubhouse would be deserted; so, he was surprised to hear the famil-iar thwack of a bat striking balls echoing around the room. When he went to investigate, he found Edgar Martinez in the underground batting cage, working on the stroke that would earn him the 1995 A.L. batting championship, his second title in four years. When Rodriguez asked him why he was still there, his team-mate had a simple answer.

"Hitting is my job," said Martinez, who retired after the 2004 season with a .312 career batting average. "And I have to put in the practice time to do it as well as I want to."

"Seeing Edgar made me realize that there were levels to the game," said Rodriguez, who had spent his after-noon relaxing, while an established veteran and batting champion had spent those same hours grooving his swing. "I knew that I needed to put in even more work than I was doing if I wanted to stay in the big leagues."

Some of the lessons that Rodriguez learned, however, were harder-earned than that one. After he had returned to the dugout following a particularly pathetic-looking strikeout, Piniella had railed at him.

"Son, you've got to give me better swings than *that*," snarled the manager, as Rodriguez put on his sunglasses to hide the tears that were welling up in his eyes. Almost instantly, however, Piniella realized that Rodriguez was doing his best, and that he probably needed a show of encouragement, rather than a public scolding; so, he walked over to his struggling shortstop and gave him a kiss on his forehead.

"In that one moment, he showed me toughness and love," recalled Rodriguez. "It meant so much to me that he cared enough to do that. Sometimes, the best lessons that we get in life come with hard edges."

Rodriguez was called up to the Mariners for the fourth and final time on August 31, which gave him a front row seat for Seattle's surprising season-ending surge. A week earlier, Griffey, who had been sidelined for most of the season with an injury, returned to a team that had been 11.5 games out of first place, and ignited the fuse for a classic stretch run that enabled the Mariners to end the season tied for first place in the American League Western Division with the Los Angeles Angels.

The Mariners, who had taken to wearing t-shirts imprinted with the motto, 'Refuse to Lose,' eliminated the Angels, 9-1, in a one-game playoff, giving the franchise its first-ever divisional title.

"Being a part of that 1995 team was an awesome experience," said Rodriguez. "I knew I wasn't ready to be a regular, but I still loved being involved in the excitement."

Their first appearance post-season looked like it would be a short-lived exercise, however, after they traveled to New York and dropped two straight games to the Yankees. But, with their backs to the wall, they returned to the Kingdome, and swept the next two games of the best-of-five series.

With the season on the line for both teams, the transcontinental rivals treated the fans in Seattle—and television viewers all around the country—to one of the most exciting post-season games in baseball history.

With the Mariners only three outs away from a 4-3 win, the Yankees rallied to tie the game with a run in the ninth, and two innings later tacked on another run, to take a 5-4 lead. The Mariners, though, lived up to the words on their t-shirts, when Edgar Martinez delivered a two-run double in the bottom of the 11th inning that scored second baseman Joey Cora and Griffey, who had raced home from first base with the winning run. As Junior streaked toward home, Rodriguez, who had entered the game in the eighth inning and was in the on-deck circle, waiting for his chance to hit, stood near the plate, pumping his palms up and down, signaling Griffey to *slide, Junior, slide*!

"It's kind of ironic, isn't it? At first I didn't want to play in Seattle," said Rodriguez, speaking in the joyous clubhouse immediately after the game. "Now I can't imagine playing anywhere else. This is the perfect place for me."

Even though the Mariners wound up losing the American League Championship Series to Cleveland, the team's exciting run had generated a great deal of optimism for the 1996 season. And it was expected that Rodriguez, given his experience and potential, would play a key role in turning those good vibes into a concrete reality.

"Alex is going to start next year," predicted Luis Sojo, who had been Seattle's shortstop, but who had also read the writing on the wall. "He has so much talent, it's unbelievable. He's like the second coming of Junior."

7   PUMPED AND HUNGRY

Although Rodriguez came to spring training in 1996 as the team's top shortstop candidate, he still had to prove that he could hit for a higher average than the anemic .232 he had posted the previous season. Piniella had counted on him to show improvement with the stick, but even he was surprised at how thoroughly the previously free-swinging Rodriguez had transformed himself into a disciplined and selective hitter.

"It came almost overnight," said Piniella, making it sound as if a wand had been waved. "It wasn't there at all one week, and, suddenly, the next week there it was. And then he just kept getting better and better."

The makeover, however, wasn't magical or sudden, and had actually begun in the off-season, when Rodriguez had studied tapes of Edgar Martinez.

"The tapes were three hours long, all his hits from the previous two seasons," explained Rodriguez, who had also worked out five days a week. "I watched them about three times a week. If you have a great hitter to learn from, it makes a lot of sense to study how they get it done."

When Rodriguez initially had trouble applying his new knowledge in spring training, he went for help from Lee Elia, who was Seattle's hitting coach.

"His swing was too long," recalled Elia. "He didn't have good bat control. We worked four, five days shortening his swing, getting him to understand that he had enough bat speed to drive the ball without taking a real long swing.

"In the first game he played after those sessions, he stroked a couple of hits. That made him feel comfortable, and he went into the season in a good frame of mind."

Early in May, after Piniella had seen that Rodriguez was for real, he moved him from the bottom of the batting order into the second slot, directly ahead of Griffey, Martinez and Jay Buhner. Hitting in front of that run-producing trio made it even easier for Rodriguez to be selective, since pitchers didn't want to take a chance on walking him before facing the dangerous hitters that followed. The move coincided with a two-month batting tear by Rodriguez, during which he hit for a .361 average and was selected as a reserve on the American League All-Star Team, behind Cal Ripken, Jr., his boyhood idol. Somewhat remarkably, knowledgeable baseball people were not only comparing Rodriguez to Ripken, but some were also starting to say that he already was or would soon be even better than the Hall of Fame-bound Baltimore shortstop.

"He's a big, physical shortstop like Ripken, but he's a better athlete," said veteran general manager John Hart, speaking of a player who was becoming known by his new nickname, *A-Rod.* "He probably has more power than Cal, and he might be a better all-around hitter."

Three weeks after he had become the youngest shortstop ever to play in an All-Star Game, the Mariners made his 21st birthday an especially happy event by signing him to a four-year, $10.5 million contract extension. Rodriguez, who had thought that he might be traded for a front-line pitcher, a commodity that was in short supply for the pitching-starved Mariners, breathed a sigh of relief after the papers were signed.

"It was a great day, an emotional day," said Rodriguez, who announced that he would use part of the money to launch a foundation, *Grand Slam for Kids*, which encourages children to work harder on reading, physical fitness, math and good citizenship. "It shows how far you can go with sacrifice, commitment and hard work."

If anyone thought that relief would lead to complacency, Rodriguez quickly dispelled that notion by going on a 20-game hitting streak, and finished the season with an American League-leading .358 average, the highest average by a right-handed hitter since Yankee Hall of Famer Joe DiMaggio batted .381 in 1939. Rodriguez, who also stroked 36 home runs and knocked in 123 runs, had produced the best season ever by a 21-year-old, and became the third-youngest player to win a batting title, after Hall of Famers Al Kaline and Ty Cobb.

"He learned in a couple of years what it took me ten years to learn," declared Edgar Martinez, who, like everyone else, had been blown away by his teammate's rapid development. "He goes with the pitch, and uses the whole field, foul pole to foul pole."

Rodriguez's outrageous hitting brought him his first Silver Slugger Award, as the League's best-hitting shortstop, and his slick fielding allowed him to finish second in the voting for the Gold Glove Award, which went to Omar Vizquel, the best-fielding shortstop of his generation. Rodriguez was also the runner-up in the voting for the league's MVP Award, finishing three votes behind

Juan Gonzalez, who was a hard-hitting, run-producing outfielder with the Texas Rangers. The decisive factor, for many of the voters, had been that Gonzalez had helped lead the Rangers to their first American League West Division championship, while the Mariners, despite Rodriguez's heroics, had finished second.

"The way he's going, someday he might bat .400 and hit 60 home runs," said veteran baseball executive Dan Duquette. "He's the best young talent I've seen for years."

Rodriguez, who had finished among the league leaders in 11 offensive categories, had compiled the most productive season by any shortstop in the history of baseball. As soon as the season ended, however, he was already looking forward to an even brighter future.

"I love the challenge of the game," said Rodriguez, whose accomplishments were made all the more sweet by the struggles that had preceded them. "I love the work. My goal right now is to have a season next year that will make people forget about this one. I'm pumped. I'm hungry."

8 SAYONARA, SEATTLE

Although many people in baseball were wondering just how high the upside was for Rodriguez, they wouldn't get the answer in 1997, because a collision that he had with Roger Clemens, who was pitching for the Toronto Blue Jays, sidelined Rodriguez for two weeks, and the bruised ribs that he suffered continued to hamper him throughout the remainder of the season.

"I came back too soon," explained Rodriguez, who still managed to become the first A.L. shortstop other than Ripken to start in an All-Star Game since 1983. "I wasn't able to throw the way I should, or swing the bat anywhere near what I'm capable of. I was playing hurt, but I wanted to be out there."

His inability to play at a hundred percent caused Rodriguez's offensive numbers to suffer a steep decline over the preceding year, although he still wound up hitting 23 homers, with 84 RBI and a .300 batting average—numbers that would have thrilled nearly every other shortstop, or any other player of Rodriguez's age and experience.

The Mariners, however, had so much firepower and pitching that they were able to overcome Rodriguez's decreased production and still take their second divisional title and register 90 wins, which was, at that time, the most in franchise history. Griffey, who was named the A.L. MVP, led the charge with 57 home runs and 147 RBI, while Martinez and Buhner combined for 68 big flies and 217 RBI. Joey Cora, first baseman Paul Sorrento and catcher Dan Wilson also played significant roles, and the team mashed a major league-record 264 home runs. Randy Johnson, who went 20-4, with a 2.28 earned run average, and 291 Ks in only 213 innings, was the dominant player on the pitching staff, and finished second behind Clemens for the Cy Young Award.

The offensive fireworks that the Mariners had produced during the regular season, unfortunately, fizzled in the Divisional Playoff series, as Baltimore's pitching staff held the power-hitting Mariners' line-up to a total of 11 runs in four games, and the Orioles romped, 3-games-to-1. All of Seattle's stars faded away during the series, except Rodriguez, who hit .312 and cracked his first post-season home run, while Ripken led all hitters with a .438 average.

"What I do as an individual has always been less important to me than what the team does," said Rodriguez, as he stood in the loser's clubhouse. "I want to help Seattle win a World Series."

The 1998 season will long be remembered as one of the most exciting in baseball history, as Mark McGwire, with 70 four-baggers, and Sammy Sosa, with 66, both eclipsed the all-time single-season home run record, which had stood at 61 since 1961, when Roger Maris had just edged past the record of 60, which had been set by Babe Ruth in 1927.

For Mariners' fans, however, 1998 will be remembered as a season of missed opportunities, and the start of an exodus that would finish with each of Seattle's three superstars—Griffey, Johnson and Rodriguez—gone by the end of the decade. It was a season that had started with great expectations in Seattle, with the fans and the team hoping to build on their accomplishments of 1997. It ended, though, as a monument to individual brilliance undermined by collective failure.

The root of the problem for the Mariners was its pitching staff, which had depended on Randy Johnson to be its ace and leader. The 6' 10" left-hander, however, was in the last year of his contract, and when he and the team couldn't agree on terms, he simply went into a funk. By the end of July, relations between the Mariners and Johnson, who had a 9-10 record and a bulging ERA, had reached a point of no return, so he was dealt to the Houston Astros.

After it became apparent that the Mariners didn't have enough overall talent to make a run at another divisional title, Seattle fans had to settle for watching the team's two remaining superstars strive to reach individual milestones. Griffey obliged by clubbing 56 home runs and swiping 20 bases, becoming only the third player to amass 50 dingers and 20 steals in a single season. Rodriguez also wrote his name into the record books by bashing 42 homers and stealing 46 bases, becoming the third player after Jose Canseco and Barry Bonds to join the 40-40 club. His home run total also eclipsed the American League record of 40 big flies by a shortstop, which had been set by Boston's Rico Petrocelli in 1969.

"Winning is the most important thing to me, so I'm disappointed that we're not going to make it to the postseason," Rodriguez told reporters after he had hit his

40th home run. "But, from an individual standpoint, reaching the 40-40 mark has to rank as the most memorable moment of my baseball career."

The Mariners moved to Safeco Field, a brand new stadium, in the middle of the 1999 season, but they ended the schedule with a 79-83 record, 16 games behind the division leader. An early-season knee injury that cost Rodriguez a chunk of games, was a serious setback for Seattle, but he came back stronger than ever and finished the season with 42 home runs and 111 RBI, in only 123 games.

"Alex has become a great player in a short time," declared Edgar Martinez. "He can run, throw, and field. He can hit for average and for power. And he's also a very mature person, who has handled fame and attention extremely well."

After the season, the Mariners complied with a request by Griffey to trade him to the Cincinnati Reds, which would allow him to play in the city in which he grew up. During the four seasons that Rodriguez and Griffey had been teammates, Junior had *averaged* 52 home runs and 141 RBI, while also winning the final four of his 10 consecutive Gold Gloves.

"He was electric," said Rodriguez, in speaking of Griffey, who had been selected by his major league peers as the Player of the Decade for the 1990s. "He'd climb outfield walls as if he was Spiderman, and I had a great seat every night. He's the best player I've ever seen on a baseball field, *period*."

With Randy Johnson and Griffey gone in successive seasons, it appeared as though Seattle might sink even farther in the standings in 2000. But Pat Gillick, who was the team's general manager, had done such a good job in overhauling the team that they looked as though they were a sure bet to win the division title, until the next-to-last weekend of the season, when they dropped 3-of-4 to the hard charging Oakland A's. As Rodriguez's slump continued through most of the final week of the season, the Mariners tumbled out of first place and, with only two games left to play, their post-season dreams appeared to be evaporating.

"Let's be honest, Alex is the heart and soul of this team," said Piniella, who was hoping that the Mariners could still catch the A's or, at least, hold off Cleveland, who was challenging them for the wild-card spot. "If he doesn't break out, we're not going to win the race to the finish line. We need Alex to get hot."

As if responding to his manager's message, Rodriguez broke out of his slump the following game, as he lashed four hits against the Angels, including his 39th and 40th home runs, the third year in a row that he had hit 40 or more big flies. The following day, they downed the Angels in another must-win game, which earned them entry into the playoffs as a wild-card team.

"I feel this was the first year I had to lead, and it was emotionally draining," explained Rodriguez, who also let it be known that he would exercise his right to become a free agent after the end of the World Series. "I know I sucked against the A's, but in the last couple of days, when our backs were against the wall, I feel proud that I somewhat answered the call."

Rodriguez continued to shoulder the load as Seattle swept three straight games from the Chicago White Sox in the Division series, but the Yankees put an end to their post-season run by taking the ALCS, 4-games-to-2.

Although he hadn't been able to lift Seattle past the collective superiority of the Yankees, Rodriguez's clutch hitting in the final weekend of the season, followed by his .371 average in the post-season, had only enhanced his value in the free-agent bazaar that was about to begin.

9 THE EYES OF TEXAS

Rodriguez had finished the 2000 season among the league leaders in virtually every offensive category and, at 25-years-old, with his prime years still in front of him, he became the most prized free agent ever.

His stated preference was to stay in Seattle, if the Mariners could show him how they planned to upgrade the team, and pay him whatever the going rate turned out to be.

"I can tell you I am seriously considering the Mariners," he explained. "But there aren't going to be any hometown discounts. I've done that before. Not this time."

Rodriguez also made it known that New York was his favorite city, and that he would welcome the opportunity to play for the Mets, who had been his favorite team while he was growing up.

"I was a *huge* Mets fan; I watched every game in '86, *Kiner's Korner,* Tim McCarver, the whole thing," said Rodriguez, referring to a post-game television show and the team's TV analyst. "My favorite player was Keith Hernandez. I *loved* him. I loved *everything* about him."

The expectation that he would sign with the Mets was raised to a fever pitch among Mets' fans when he showed up at Yankee Stadium to watch the Bronx Bombers play against the Mets in the 2000 World Series. Alex insisted that he had come just to cheer on his friend,

Derek Jeter. But, while Alex told that tale to the media, the story that he told his friends was that he was hoping to sign with the Mets for 10 years, and around $190 million.

It seemed like a perfect match between a player who wanted to play on the biggest stage, and a team from the biggest of all markets, which needed a great player to compete on the field, and a marquee name to draw fans and television viewers, as well as to sell merchandise.

The Mets, however, unexpectedly stepped aside, and the Mariners didn't step up to the plate with what Rodriguez and his agent, Scott Boras, considered to be a suitable plan or enough dollars, Rodriguez accepted an extraordinary offer from Tom Hicks, the owner of the Texas Rangers: *a $252 million dollar, ten-year contract, which was more than twice as much money as any baseball player had ever been guaranteed.*

The numbers were so staggering that there wasn't really any rational frame of reference in which to view them. Although he was thrilled about signing his name on the bottom line, Rodriguez realized the contract was, by any measure, outsized.

"It's almost embarrassing to talk about," acknowledged Rodriguez. "I don't know if Michael Jordan, or Bill Gates, or *Alexander the Great*, or *anyone* is worth this type of money, but that's the market we're in today. That's what Mr. Hicks decided to pay me, and now it's time to pay him back and win a couple of championships."

Although he delivered more than anyone could have expected, and established himself as the best player in the American League during the three seasons that he spent in Texas, his astonishing accomplishments weren't enough to help lead the always pitching-poor Rangers out of the divisional cellar in any one of those seasons, let alone lead the team to a championship.

Rodriguez was able to deflect the pressure that the outsized contract had placed on him and deliver big time in 2001, as he went on to lead the league with 52 dingers and 133 runs scored, and finished third in RBI (135) and slugging percentage (.622), while hitting .318.

Although most people use statistics as the prime measure for evaluating performance, Rodriguez judges himself on what he does to put himself in a position to produce.

"I don't base my goals on numbers," he explained. "All my goals are based on my work ethic and my preparation. Those are the only things that I can control."

Meanwhile, no one could have blamed Rodriguez if he had turned an envious and regretful eye towards the northwest, where Japanese import Ichiro Suzuki, who was named Rookie of the Year and MVP, helped lead a reconfigured Seattle team to an American League record, with 116 wins.

If Rodriguez had needed a hint at how the season would play out, he received it when he returned to Seattle as one of only two Rangers' representatives for the 2001 All-Star Game that featured *eight* Mariners. Although Rodriguez continued to receive the jeers that the Seattle fans had been showering on him since his first visit to Safeco in April, he took special delight in witnessing Cal Ripken hitting a home run in his last appearance in an All-Star Game.

In 2002, Rodriguez took his game to an even higher

level, as he led the majors in RBI (142) and home runs (57), to become only the fifth player ever to hit 50 big flies in back-to-back seasons. He also won the first of his two consecutive Gold Glove Awards for fielding excellence, clearly staking his claim to being the game's best all-around player.

"He's the best player I've ever seen," said Rangers' manager Buck Showalter, an opinion that was shared by a great many baseball people. "He does everything: hit, field and run, at the very highest level. And he's also a great leader, who does everything that he can to help our younger players."

Rafael Palmeiro, who slugged 43 four-baggers and drove in 105 runs, and catcher Ivan Rodriguez, also did their parts to try to lift Texas out of last place. But the rest of the roster was littered with mediocre journeymen and young players—such as second baseman Michael Young and third baseman Hank Blalock—who weren't yet ready to deliver prime-time performances.

Although Rodriguez couldn't extract much joy from playing on a losing baseball team, he did have the best off-season of his life because, on November 2nd, he married Cynthia Scurtis, a high school psychology teacher.

"The day I got married was the most memorable day of my life," said Rodriguez. "The next one will be the day my first child is born. That will be the most special day in my life."

His wife has also used her training in psychology to help Rodriguez and his father start to reconcile with one another, which also led to Rodriguez getting together with his older half-brother, someone he hadn't seen since he was four years old.

"Any time your father isn't around, there is a void," said Cynthia, who made a phone call to Victor to get the process started. "When I met Alex I felt he owed it to himself to find out and make his own judgment as an adult."

"As a kid you want everything to be perfect, and you don't understand the nature of divorce," said Rodriguez, who came to realize that there were issues between his parents that he wasn't aware of. "With Cynthia's help, I was able to understand that many relationships don't work out. She gave me the courage to get things going."

But, try as he might, Rodriguez wasn't able to get anything going in Texas, even though he tied for the major league lead in home runs in 2003, and finished among the league leaders in virtually every major hitting category.

His individual exploits earned him the AL MVP Award, making him only the second player ever from a last place team to win a league MVP Award, but he had grown weary of all the losing and told Tom Hicks that he wanted to be traded. Piling up huge stats and winning individual awards didn't mean very much to him anymore, without the challenge of playing for a team that could, at least, contend for a championship.

10 BACK TO THE BEGINNING

Rodriguez and Texas owner Tom Hicks had come together with the best of intentions but, after three fruitless seasons, they had both come to realize that it was time to separate. Hicks had learned that a lone superstar can't single-handedly transform a team, and that giving so much money to one player can limit what one has left to spend on getting complementary players. Rodriguez, meanwhile, had learned that even hundreds of millions of dollars isn't payment enough for being on a team that doesn't even have a chance of being competitive.

"It's a lot easier to play well when you're having fun, and winning is obviously a lot more fun than losing," Rodriguez explained to reporters. "Last season was the toughest of my career because of that. I was overcome with a sense of depression. There were days I didn't want to go to the ballpark. That had never happened to me before."

Rodriguez had certainly lived up to his side of the bargain by *averaging* 52 home runs and 132 RBI, while posting three of the best seasons that any player has ever strung together.

"Alex was our leader," said Hicks, who had accepted the fact that it was time to trade Rodriguez and try to build the team differently. "He was always coming up with ideas of how he thought the team could be improved. He always encouraged and helped our younger players. Alex played his heart out for three years."

Rodriguez was so determined to play for a contender that he offered to take a substantial cut in salary as part of a deal that would have sent him to Boston for Red Sox slugger Manny Ramírez. The Players Association, however, ruled that the amount of money that Rodriguez would have had to rescind to the Red Sox was a violation of baseball's collective bargaining agreement, so the trade was cancelled.

Rodriguez was devastated by that decision and the prospect of being stuck in Texas for another season with the Rangers. Shortly before the start of spring training, however, Rodriguez was traded to the Yankees for All-Star second baseman, Alfonso Soriano. Rodriguez was so happy to be returning to the city of his birth and to play for a perennial contender, that he agreed to switch from shortstop to third base, since the Yankees' shortstop position was already manned by its captain, Derek Jeter.

"I grew up with a Cal Ripken, Jr. poster over my bed, and I wanted to reach certain goals as a shortstop, but that doesn't matter to me anymore," said a jubilant Rodriguez. "I'm more interested in the prospect of winning a championship, and I'm looking forward to the new challenge."

His arrival in New York also delighted the large Dominican population, especially those in Washington Heights, where Rodriguez had been born.

"You're talking about the Latin Babe Ruth," declared Miguel Montás, the owner of a neighborhood Dominican restaurant, El Nuevo Caridad, which is often frequented by Dominican players when they're in New

York. "The Latin people have a message today to Yankees' owner, George Steinbrenner: Thank you for doing this for us."

"I have never seen Alex so happy," said Eddie Rodriguez, the Boys and Girls Club director, who remains one of A-Rod's closest friends. "He's in the best shape of his life. When the Yankee deal happened, he was like a little kid he was so excited."

Putting on the pinstriped uniform and playing in Yankee Stadium, the most hallowed field in baseball, presents unique challenges, however. There's the daunting history of excellence, exemplified by the 26 World Series banners, the long list of Hall of Fame players, and revered retired numbers that are also displayed. A-Rod, in fact, had to switch the number on his jersey from '3' to '13', since the great Babe Ruth had worn the lower number. And the entire organization, from the owner to the players, judged the success of each season by only one criterion: Winning the World Series.

"You're not paid to win 100 games here," explained team executive and Hall of Famer Reggie Jackson, who had earned the nickname "Mr. October," for his post-season exploits with the Yankees. "You're not paid to take us from 102 wins to 109. *You're paid to win the last 11.*"

Rodriguez, of course, would have loved to start the 2004 season with a hot streak, which would have allowed him to settle in and reach a comfort zone with his new teammates. Instead, he got off to the coldest start of his career, flailing at pitches the way he did when he first came up to the big leagues.

"That was the first time in my career I felt *totally*

helpless, totally out of control," said Rodriguez, who posted a .160 average through his first 50 at-bats. "I wasn't ready for that, and I didn't like that feeling *at all*."

Rodriguez may have felt the pressure of playing for a contending team for the first time since he had left Seattle, or maybe it had something to do with playing a new position, or at Yankee Stadium, or in New York, the country's biggest fish bowl.

"A lot of times I feel like a rookie here," said Rodriguez. "My biggest adjustment has been to control my emotions and realize that while every game's important, we're not at the seventh game of the World Series, yet."

Joe Torre, who was the Yankees' manager, did what he could to try to get Rodriguez to ease up on himself, take deep breaths, and to just allow his natural ability to take over.

"When he goes up to the plate, he expects magic to happen all the time," said Torre. "That's very tough to live up to. Some players need to dial up their intensity, with Alex it's just the opposite."

Eventually, Rodriguez did manage to dig himself out of the hole he had dug earlier in the season, and wound up hitting .286, with 35 homers and 108 RBI, but he hit only .248 with runners in scoring position, and his productivity wasn't up to the standard that he had set in his previous seven seasons.

"Nothing has been easy this year," he acknowledged, right before the Yankees—who had finished the regular season in their usual spot atop the AL East standings—opened the playoffs with a series against the Minnesota Twins. "But I feel like my best baseball is ahead of me."

Rodriguez did, in fact, play his best ball of the season against the Twins, as he hit .421 and led the Yankees to a 3-games-to-1 win over Minnesota. Rodriguez had it all working in the 11th inning of Game 4, when he stroked a double off reliever Kyle Lohse, stole third, and then scored the winning run when the unhinged Lohse threw a wild pitch.

"When you think you've seen everything he can do, he continues to amaze you," said Gary Sheffield, who was the Yankees' right fielder. "He's the best player in the game, and he showed that tonight."

Rodriguez continued to pound the ball during the first three games against Boston, the Yankees' keenest rival, in the American League Championship Series. But then, as if a door had been slammed, he suddenly stopped hitting. The other Yankee bats also went cold, and the Red Sox staged a stunning comeback by sweeping the next four games, and becoming the first major league team to overcome a 0-3 deficit in the post-season.

"Nothing came easy this year," said Rodriguez. "But we'll be back next year, and the year after that. I know I'll have the chance to play for a championship every season, and that's all I can ask for."

Rodriguez bounced back big-time in 2005, as he finished among the top five in the league in all the important offensive categories, while also picking up his second A.L. MVP Award. The post-season, however, was a different matter, as Rodriguez had a 2-for-15 meltdown, as the Yankees were downed by the Angels in the opening round, 3-games-to-2.

"I can't wait to get to spring training to work on my skills, continue to become a better player and reach my ultimate goal," said Rodriguez, whose delight in winning the award was tempered by his failure to ignite any post-season fireworks. "Winning the MVP is a great accomplishment, but I'm here to do one thing, which is to win a World Series."

As it turned out, Rodriguez didn't become a better player in 2006. He struggled early in the regular season, both at the plate and in the field, where he wound up tying his career high with 24 errors. Although he found his stroke later in the season, and wound up with a respectable .290 average and 121 RBI, he hacked only 35 home runs, the least he had hit since 1997, when he missed 21 games and played most of the season with bruised ribs. He also didn't make it to the World Series, as the Yankees were again eliminated in the opening round of post-season play, 3-games-to-1, by the Detroit Tigers, and Rodriguez had another flameout in the play-offs.

"I stunk," admitted Rodriguez, who was dropped to the 8th spot in the batting order in Game 4 by Joe Torre. "I went 1-for-14, with an error, and that's disappointing and embarrassing. But I'll work as hard as I can to get ready for 2007, and we'll see what happens then."

Although no one has ever questioned A-Rod's work ethic, his lack of production in post-season play did start to draw the scorn of a large segment of the media, especially in New York, as well as large numbers of Yankee fans, who actually booed him at times.

In part, everyone seems outraged that someone who earns as much money as A-Rod makes doesn't deliver *all* the time; an attitude that seems to be based on financial jealousy and unreasonable expectations. A great many fans in New York have always seemed to have, at best, an ambivalent attitude toward Rodriguez, who doesn't seem to fit their ideal of what it is to be a *real* Yankee, the way the iconic Derek Jeter does.

In fact, a rupture in the relationship between Jeter and Rodriguez, which occurred in 2001, when A-Rod said some critical things about Jeter's abilities, is probably a partial explanation for the fans' reaction to Rodriguez. Although A-Rod has frequently tried to apologize to Jeter for his comments, which appeared in Esquire magazine, the close personal relationship has never been restored. And Jeter, although he is the team captain, has never tried to intercede with the fans on his teammate's behalf, and ask them to stop their senseless and harmful booing of Rodriguez.

Although both players had always told inquiring reporters that everything was fine in their relationship, Rodriguez finally set the record straight at the start of spring training for the 2007 season.

"Let's make a contract," said Rodriguez. "You don't ask me any more questions about Derek, and I promise that I'll stop lying about it. The reality is that the nature of our relationship has changed. But it's not a big deal. We're on the same page. We're here to win a championship together."

Acknowledging the fissure in his relationship seemed to relax Rodriguez, and he went on to lead the majors with 156 RBI and 54 home runs, and earn his third A.L. MVP Award in the past five seasons. His production was the major reason that the Yankees were able to make it into the playoffs as a wild-card team. But, in what has become a familiar story, they were eliminated in the first round, 3-games-to-1, by Cleveland, and while A-Rod's hitting didn't disappear, it wasn't any better than mediocre.

After the season, Rodriguez opted out of his contract with the Yankees, but then quickly decided to sign a new deal with the team.

Although A-Rod has, without question, made some mistakes and has sometimes slumped when the games mean the most, it's never been for lack of trying, and he has never offered up excuses, or whined about the negative reaction he's received.

"I have a lot to prove in New York," acknowledged A-Rod, who has 518 career home runs, and is on pace to shatter the all-time home run record of 762, which is held by Barry Bonds. "I still have unfinished business to attend to."

Given another opportunity to crash a post-season party, A-Rod could very well put on a record-breaking show that would be as great as anything that he or anyone else has ever done and, maybe, silence some of his noisy critics.

"As good as he is, he still has growth potential," noted Reggie Jackson. "He's had some problems, but that's part of the growth process. And let's put this in perspective, A-Rod's on a pace with the greatest players in the history of the game. He hasn't gotten there yet, but he deserves the recognition for being where he is. One day his record will compare to the legacies of Ruth, Lou Gehrig and all the great Yankee players of the past."

ALEX RODRIGUEZ

Born: July 27, 1975, in New York City, New York
Height: 6-3   Weight: 225   MLB Seasons: 13

CAREER STATS

Games	AB	R	H	HR	RBI	OBP	SLG	AVG
1,904	7,350	1,501	2,250	518	1,503	.389	.578	.306

67

ALBERT PUJOLS

Born: January 16, 1980, in Santo Domingo, Dominican Republic
Height: 6-3   Weight: 230   MLB Seasons: 7

CAREER STATS

Games	AB	R	H	HR	RBI	OBP	SLG	AVG
1,091	4,054	847	1,344	282	861	.420	.620	.332

1   IN THE BEGINNING

Jose Alberto Pujols came into the world on January 16, 1980, in Santo Domingo, the capital city of the Dominican Republic.

Historically, the Dominican Republic was the first site in the Western Hemisphere to be permanently colonized by European explorers and conquerors, starting with Christopher Columbus. While the four arduous and dangerous journeys that Columbus made to the West involved unquestioned acts of bravery, his greed in plundering the land's resources and his brutal treatment and enslavement of the native peoples he encountered set an example that would, sadly, be too well followed by those who came after him.

Geographically, the Dominican Republic sits slightly less than 700 miles southeast of Key West, Florida, and just over 150 miles west of Puerto Rico, where it is nestled in the balmy, blue waters of the Caribbean. The DR, where Spanish is the official language, occupies two-thirds of the island of Hispaniola, while the other third is occupied by Haiti, a French-speaking country, which has suffered through decades of unending political and social instability, despotic and dysfunctional governments, and the greatest level of poverty in the Western hemisphere.

Although the DR has, in recent years, benefited from

stable and democratic government, and its degree of poverty isn't nearly as extreme as Haiti's, the majority of its citizens still live in such a precarious economic state that necessities such as food, housing and healthcare are not items to be taken for granted. For many Dominicans, three meals a day are not a given, while the purchase of sports equipment that most children in the U.S. take for granted, such as a baseball glove and bat, are luxuries beyond the reach of a large percentage of the population in the DR.

Despite the handicap of poverty and the lack of equipment, baseball did manage to gain a toehold in the DR, and has gone on to become such a hotbed of fan involvement that it has become one of the few countries in the world, besides the US, where baseball is more popular than soccer. The country has its own professional league of six teams, whose schedule runs from October to January. The Winter League, as it is known, is filled mostly with homegrown players who don't have the ability to make the jump north to the Major Leagues. But the rosters are always dotted with a sprinkling of Dominican players, both established big leaguers and minor league hopefuls, who return from their summer stints in the U.S. and welcome the opportunity to perform in front of their hometown fans.

The first player from the Dominican Republic to make it to the big leagues was Ozzie Virgil, Sr., who had moved to New York City with his family in 1947, the same year that Jackie Robinson became the first black person to be allowed to play in the major leagues. Virgil began his big league career with the then-New York

Giants on September 23, 1956 by going 0-for-4 against the Philadelphia Phillies.

"Tough day," recalled Virgil, who is a special instructor for the New York Mets, and who still displays the buoyancy that has endeared him to so many people for such a long time. "But I got better the next day. I got five hits."

Although Virgil, who compiled a .231 career average while playing for six teams in nine big league seasons, had many more bad days at the plate than good ones, he was, more importantly, a pioneer who set an example and paved the way for the Latino players who have followed in the trail that he initially blazed.

"I'm glad that he was first because he is such a good person and we needed the first to be somebody special," said New York Yankees' coach Tony Pena who, like Virgil, was born in the town of Monte Christi. "He is full of charisma and always has a smile on his face. He is a hero to all of us."

Two years after his debut with the Giants, Virgil was involved in another historical moment when, after a trade to Detroit, he became the first dark-skinned player to play for the Tigers.

"I had a lot of fun, I played every position but pitcher in the Major Leagues, and I was very fortunate to play as long as I did," said Virgil, a journeyman who never played more than 96 games or had more than 226 at-bats in a season. "I know there were players who could have done better than I did, but I knew that I was making history. I had a mission to accomplish, which was to do something for my country."

Given the opportunity to perform in the big leagues, players from Latin America soon showed that they could excel at the highest level and even gain entrance to the Baseball Hall of Fame. Puerto Rican-born Roberto Clemente, who won four batting titles for the Pittsburgh Pirates in the 1960s, became the first Latino to gain entrance into the Hall of Fame, when he was elected with the Class of 1973. Ten years later, former San Francisco Giants' hurler Juan Marichal, who was nicknamed the Dominican Dandy, became the first Latino pitcher to earn a plaque in Cooperstown.

The signing of Virgil had started a trickle of baseball talent moving north from the DR and other Latin countries, and that trickle quickly turned into a torrent, until now there are more players from the Dominican Republic in the big leagues than there are from any other country, except the United States, while Latino players, overall, make up about 25 percent of all major league players.

The players from the DR don't merely populate major league teams; they often dominate the game with a constantly growing list of All-Stars and probable Hall of Famers, which includes the likes of Sammy Sosa, who has hammered more home runs than any other Latino player, David Ortiz, Vladimir Guerrero, Jose Reyes, Miguel Tejada, Pedro Martínez and Manny Ramírez. While players from other Latin American countries, such as Panama's Mariano Rivera, Puerto Rico's Ivan Rodriguez and Venezuela's Johan Santana are perennial All-Stars who are on course for eventual induction in Cooperstown.

"Sometimes, I wonder if today's players even know what we went through and the problems that we had with the color barrier," said Virgil, who has gone on to manage teams in Latin America and coach for several big league teams. "I'm happy for the players and the fact that they make lots of money and get to help their families. But I wonder if they ever stop to think about what it was like for the players who were on the front lines back in the day.

"The most important message I have for the younger generation is to go to school and get an education. Be good citizens and keep up the good work. Let's keep the Dominican Republic on the map and be good examples for players coming up. That's what I tried to do."

Virgil's historic breakthrough eventually led big league teams to hire Latinos as coaches, managers and front office executives, like Omar Minaya, the general manager of the New York Mets.

"All of us are indebted to Ozzie," said Minaya, who was born in the Dominican Republic. "Not only was he the first, but he helped many of the others who came after him. He helped bridge the gap between the young Spanish-speaking players and their new teammates, coaches and managers. And he was not only a player; he extended his influence by going on to become a coach and a manager, as well. We owe him a lot."

2 BIG LEAGUE DREAMS

Albert Pujols was born into the poverty typical of the population of the Dominican Republic, and without the benefit of having his parents in his daily life. His father, Bienvenido, who was a well-regarded pitcher in his day, was often away from his son, seeking work, and his mother wasn't able to care for her child. Because Pujols doesn't speak publicly about his mother, she's become a shadowy mystery, but there are rumors that suggest that she suffers from serious emotional problems.

Luckily for Pujols, he had a loving, extended family, which filled the void created by his parents' absences. Chief among those relatives was his grandmother, America, who essentially raised him, and an uncle, one of America's 11 children, Antonio Joaquin dos Santos, in whose home Pujols lived for seven years.

When Pujols began playing pick-up baseball games as an eight-year-old, he couldn't afford a baseball glove or a bat, so he did what generations of Dominicans have done before and after him: he cut a milk carton into the shape of a mitt, grabbed a stick and made do as best as he could.

Eventually, his relatives were able to supply Pujols with some equipment and, more importantly, gave him the encouragement and support that would, in time, help propel him into professional baseball.

"My family did whatever they could to help me get a pair of spikes or batting gloves," recalled Albert, who soon began to dream of becoming one of the lucky few with enough talent to become a major league player. "It's because of their support that I was able to make it to the big leagues."

Back then, no one actually thought that Pujols was on his way to any substantial success on the diamond, let alone on a path that would take him to the major leagues. Although he had benefited from some expert coaching from his father, Pujols hadn't been a childhood prodigy or a teen-age sensation in the DR, where major league teams are allowed to sign players to contracts when they turn 16 years of age. But not a single big league scout showed up at Pujols' doorstep on his sixteenth birthday, or expressed any interest in signing him.

In 1996, during the summer after his sixteenth birthday, Pujols moved to the United States, along with his grandmother and father. Like tens of millions of other immigrants who have come to this country, Bienvenido was hoping to build a better life for himself and his family. Their first stop was the Washington Heights section of New York City, which is home to the largest population of Dominicans in the U.S. Their stay in NYC was a short one, however, because the size and pace of the Big Apple overwhelmed them, and they quickly decided to move to Independence, Missouri, a small Midwestern town, which is located a few miles east of Kansas City. To the extent that people outside of Missouri have heard of Independence at all, it is most likely because it was the childhood home of Harry S. Truman, who was the thirty-third President of the United States.

The move to the U.S. involved a lot more than merely the distance traveled for Pujols. He was, suddenly, a stranger in a foreign town, needing to acclimate himself to a new culture, and unable to communicate with very many people, because he spoke very little English. He had gone from living with a large extended family, in a neighborhood filled with friends whom he had spent his entire life with, to living in a town in which he didn't know anyone except his two immediate relatives, and nearly nobody spoke the language that had been his native tongue for his entire life.

Because he couldn't speak English, Pujols had to register at Fort Osage High School as a sophomore, instead of as a junior, which was the grade he would have been assigned to had he stayed in the DR. Instead of being discouraged by the necessity of learning a new language, while also keeping up with the normal class work, Pujols worked as hard at mastering English as he did at bashing baseballs.

"He was a very willing student," said Portia Stanke, who was Albert's language tutor during the two-and-a-half years that he spent at Fort Osage High School. "He was dedicated about learning the language, and always very well prepared."

When Pujols went to try out for the high school baseball team the following February, he also showed Dave Fry, the school's baseball coach, that he was prepared to add a big bat to the team's line-up.

"The first time he took some swings, I was running a fielding drill, and not even watching him," recalled Fry, as he smiled at the recollection. "But the sound of the bat on the ball certainly caught my attention, and made me turn around to see who it was that was generating that thump. The sound was explosive, like the crack of thunder, and it was just as startling. I just looked at him and thought, 'He looks like a man playing against boys.'"

Pujols was named the team's starting shortstop, and even though his English vocabulary was still very limited, he and coach Fry didn't have any trouble communicating with each other.

"Even though I didn't speak Spanish and Albert hadn't, as yet, become fluent in English, I was always able to communicate exactly what I wanted him to do," said coach Fry. "Whether it was how I wanted him to position himself in the field, or how to move his hands when he was at bat, there was never a problem. He held the bat a bit higher than I thought was optimum, and I suggested that he lower his hands a little. That was about as far as it went. He had such a deep understanding of the game that I didn't have to do a great deal of instructing. He had, obviously, had some good coaching in the DR, and he just seemed to be a natural-born baseball player."

Although Pujols had benefited from good coaching and was lucky to have been born with a high degree of natural talent, neither of those factors would have mattered if he hadn't been willing to put in countless hours of practice time to hone his talent and refine the techniques that he'd been taught.

With Pujols leading the way with a .471 average, 11 home runs, and 32 RBI, Fort Osage romped to the 1997 Missouri Class 4A championship.

"That was an amazing feeling, to come to America and help my team win a championship that first year," recalled Pujols. It doesn't get much better than that."

Ironically, the outsized success that Pujols had enjoyed limited his production the following spring, as opposing coaches frequently had their pitchers walk him, rather than provide him the opportunity to wreak destruction with his bat. In his 88 at-bats in the spring of 1998, Pujols drew an astonishing 55 bases-on-balls, a situation which would frustrate any player, especially a young one trying to make his mark. But Pujols showed the same discipline at the plate then that he does now, and he refused to go fishing after balls thrown out of the strike zone.

"Opposing coaches took the bat out his hands, and I knew, as competitive as he is, how much that annoyed him," noted Fry. "But unlike most young players—and even a lot of professional ones—Albert didn't allow pitchers to expand his strike zone. If they didn't throw strikes, Albert took the walk."

Remarkably, Pujols kept his stroke, despite seeing so few strikes, and averaged one home run for every four at-bats, which showed that the fear of opposing coaches was justified. What made Pujols seem special, in addition to just his numbers, was the incredible power that he displayed. Some of the home runs that he hit are as alive in Fry's memory as though they happened yesterday, especially one that would have traveled out of most major league stadiums, with room to spare.

"He hit the ball so hard, so high that it cleared the left field fence and landed on top of an air conditioning unit that was on the roof of a building," recalled Fry. "That ball had to travel 450 feet, and while it was in the air, I didn't think it was ever going to come down."

3   NO SURE THING

Although Pujols had demonstrated prime-time power, he barely created a blip on the radar screen of most major league scouts, who were concerned about the high amount of errors that he had made at shortstop and his reputed lack of speed going from home to first.

"He certainly had the size and strength," noted Mike Roberts, a scout for the St. Louis Cardinals. "But he was by no means the type of player that had a 'can't-miss' tag on him."

A number of people advised Pujols to graduate as quickly as he could from high school so that he could enroll in a junior college for the spring 1999 season. The thinking was that he would just be wasting his time playing another season of high school baseball, since prep school pitchers had shown that they didn't want any part of him. And if he didn't get the chance to swing the bat, he wouldn't be able to create a favorable impression with major league scouts.

Pujols followed that sensible advice, and was able to enroll in Maple Woods Community College, a few miles away from his home in Kansas City.

It took all of one batting practice session for Pujols to convince Landon Brandes, who was a year ahead of Pujols and regarded as the team's best hitter, that there was a new top dog in town.

"I was feeling pretty good about my session," said Brandes. "I put more than a few balls over the fence but, like everyone else, I was using an aluminum bat. Then Albert steps in, using a wooden bat, and proceeds to hit balls that made my blasts look skimpy. It was a humbling moment."

While Brandes may have been humbled to realize the size of the power gap that existed between Pujols and himself, he was delighted to have the freshman's hard-hitting bat in the Centaurs' lineup.

"After watching Albert blast ball after ball into the great beyond, I realized that we had the ability to make a run at a title," said Brandes. "It was obvious that he would add a new dimension to our offense."

Pujols started to vindicate his teammate's judgment in the Centaurs' season opener, when he turned an unassisted triple play and smacked a grand slam far over the left field fence.

"Talk about getting off on the right foot," said Marty Kilgore, the Maple Woods' baseball coach. "Albert certainly started the season with a bang. It didn't take a certified genius to realize that we had someone special."

As it turned out his performance in that first game set the tone for what turned out to be a monster, record-setting season for Pujols, who went on to hammer 22 home runs and rack up 76 RBI in only 56 games, while posting an eye-popping .466 batting average and a .953 slugging percentage, all of which set single-season school records.

"He obviously had tremendous power and a great eye, but it wasn't just his hitting that impressed me," recalled Kilgore. "He was an excellent and aggressive base-runner, who knew how and when to take an extra base. He did all the little things that are telltale signs of exceptional baseball intelligence. He was, without a doubt, the finest athlete I've ever seen or coached."

With Pujols leading the way, Maple Woods was able to take home the 1999 National Junior College Athletic Association regional championship, and fell only one game short of making it to the Junior College World Series.

Although Pujols had put up awesome numbers and was eligible for the 1999 Major League draft that June, most of the scouts who had watched him didn't think that he had what it takes to make it in professional baseball. In that chorus of doubters rose one countervailing voice, that of Fernando Arango, who was, at the time, a scout for the Tampa Bay Devil Rays.

"What I saw in him was tremendous athletic ability," said Arango. "He just hit the ball with an impact that you don't see every day. I went to a game at Maple Woods when he cracked two home runs, and the sound of the bat on the balls sounded like cannon shots."

Arango's rapturous reports convinced Dan Jennings, who was team's scouting director, to fly Pujols in for a pre-draft tryout at Tampa Bay's home park, Tropicana Field. But Pujols didn't do anything to impress the Tampa Bay staff, let alone live up to Arango's high rating.

"He didn't put a single ball into the stands, and only one even reached the warning track," remembered Jennings. "He didn't do anything to indicate that he could even make the majors, let alone become a great player."

On draft day, every team passed up Pujols until the

13th round, when the St. Louis Cardinals finally called his name, but only after 401 other players had already been picked ahead of him. Arango became so upset at Tampa Bay's refusal to take his advice about Pujols that he resigned his job with the team.

"I was so frustrated," recalled Arango, who went on to become the coordinator of Latin American Scouting for the Milwaukee Brewers. "To me it was very simple: If I can't get a guy like that, even in the 10th round, maybe I need to be somewhere where my recommendations are more respected."

The decision to believe what his eyes told him and ignore his scout's advice quickly came back to haunt Jennings, who went on to become the Player Personnel Director of the Florida Marlins. But the lost opportunity also taught him a valuable lesson, which is to put more weight on the advice of scouts who are passionate about the prospects who they see repeatedly, rather than relying on a single workout to make player decisions.

"That was absolutely the biggest mistake we made when I was in Tampa Bay," acknowledged Jennings. "For a while, I just thought I was hexed. Every time I'd turn on a TV when he came up with the Cardinals he would be hitting a home run or driving in the winning run. I'd look up and say, 'I get the message.' You can make one bad decision and it can bite you forever. If we had picked him even as low as the ninth round, we'd look like geniuses."

Being picked so low was not the end of Pujols' disappointment with being drafted. He was further irritated when the club only offered him a $10,000 signing bonus.

It bothered him so much, in fact, that he even thought about giving up his dream of becoming a big league baseball player.

"It made me feel as though they had no respect for my ability," said Pujols. "I was so disappointed that I even thought about quitting baseball."

But after he stepped back and took a few deep breaths, Pujols decided to play in the Jayhawk League, a summer league for college-aged players, and he did so well that by the end of the season the Cardinals had raised their offer all the way up to $65,000, which included salary for the 2000 season, a signing bonus and money set aside for Albert to continue his college studies. To this day, Pujols has used his draft-day disappointment and that first contract offer as fuel to prove all the skeptics wrong.

"All that stays with him, absolutely," noted Scott Mihlfeld, a friend and trainer who works with Albert in the off-season. "Albert is a hard-headed guy. He does not forget. He doesn't hold grudges, but there is no question that being drafted low and having the Cardinals come in with a low-ball offer motivates him every day."

4   A ONE-MAN WRECKING CREW

Once Pujols had signed his initial contract with the Cardinals, he wisely decided to concentrate on his future and put the past to rest. He knew that from here on, he would be judged on what he did going forward, and not stale evaluations of what he had done earlier.

"I realized that it didn't really matter how I was rated at the time," said Pujols, who had just wanted to start climbing up the Cardinals' minor league ladder. "I knew if I was good enough, I would make it to the big leagues in three or four years."

Pujols, who knew that it usually took a prospect three to four years to work his way up to the big leagues, took his first step in the fall of 1999, when he joined the Cardinals' Instructional League team in Jupiter, Florida. But it took only a few days of bashing balls over fences for Pujols to impress Cardinals' executive Mike Jorgensen, and make him scratch his head about the low grades that scouts had given the young slugger.

"I know that some of them had doubts about his speed and physique, but it didn't take a telescope to see that his bat speed was exceptional," recalled Jorgensen, a former big league first baseman and manager. "Everyone missed the boat on Albert, and we were just lucky to have anchored him in the 13th round. In fact, we would have been lucky and looked a whole lot smarter if we had picked Prince Albert in the first round."

During the short season of Instructional League play the Cardinals switched Pujols to third base, where his limited range wouldn't be the handicap it is for a short-stop. He adapted well to his new position and was, as always, productive with the stick. During the winter, Pujols returned home to work out and earn money at a part-time job. The highlight moment of his first off-season in professional baseball occurred, without question, on the first day of the new millennium when Pujols married Deidre, a woman he had been dating for the previous year. He also adopted Deidre's infant daughter, Isabella, who had been born with Down syndrome, a genetic abnormality.

Although he was only 19 years old at the time, the responsibility of becoming a father to a child with special needs was never an issue for Pujols.

"I never really gave it a thought," said Pujols, who has gone on to have two other children with his wife. "I loved Deidre and I loved Isabella. It was as simple as that."

The following month, Pujols went to work for the Cardinals' low-level Class-A team in the Midwest League, and his hitting and work ethic made a positive impression on his manager, Tom Lawless, a former big league infielder.

"He needed to work on his defense, which he did with great diligence, but it was clear from the get-go that he was a superior hitter," recalled Lawless. "For one thing, he had great mechanics, and he also seemed mature beyond his years. Most power hitters, especially young ones, try to pull everything, no matter where the pitch is thrown. But whenever Albert got a pitch from the middle of the plate on out, he would go with the pitch and hit the ball to right or right center.

"After the other teams figured out what he was about, they had their pitchers try to get him out by jamming him with inside pitches. That was effective for a short time, but we taught him how to generate more bat speed through the strike zone and, in no time, he was turning on those inside pitches and racking up extra-base hits to left and left center. At that point, it must have been pretty discouraging to be standing on the mound when Albert stepped into the batter's box. With his strong hands and his extraordinary eye-hand coordination, he's just a devastating hitter."

What made Pujols stand out even more was the way that he reacted to his early success. Instead of feeling satisfied, he became determined to raise the bar to an even higher level. When Mitchell Page, who was the Cardinals' roving minor league hitting instructor came to Peoria, Pujols was the first player to seek his advice.

"He wasn't happy hitting just because he was hitting over .300, so I gave him all the extra work he wanted," said Page, who quickly saw that he was working with an extraordinary talent. "But he was already an A+ student, and I really didn't have too much more knowledge of the art of hitting than he already had. Which, when you stop to think about it, is a pretty amazing comment to be able to make about a player in his first minor league season."

Pujols, who was chosen as the Midwest League's All-

Star third baseman, went on to play 109 games for Peoria, during which he hit for a .324 average, while hammering 17 big flies and driving in 84 runners, while striking out only 37 times in 395 at-bats. He also led the league in slugging percentage, and finished second in batting and fourth in extra-base hits.

"Once he figured it out—and he figured it real fast—there wasn't any doubt, at least not in my mind, that he would hit in the big leagues," said Lawless.

Although anyone with eyes could see what Pujols could do with a bat in his strong hands, the people who played with him every day saw that there was more to him and his game than just his powerful stroke.

"Everyone who saw Albert play knew that he was a special talent," said Albert's Peoria teammate, Ben Johnson, a fourth round pick by the Cardinals in the 1999 draft, who was soon traded to the San Diego Padres, and is currently in the New York Mets organization. "He was a great third baseman—the best in the league we played in, *by far*. A lot of people don't know how good an athlete Albert is. He can play basketball, too. He can do anything, really. More importantly, he was a wonderful teammate."

After the season was over, Baseball America named Pujols the Midwest League's best batting prospect, top defensive third baseman, and the owner of the best arm among the league's infielders. He was also named the league's MVP, even though he had missed the last month of their season.

In August, the Cards decided to promote Pujols to their higher level Class-A team in the Carolina league. In his brief stint with the Virginia-based Cannons, Pujols hit .284 in 21 games and showed that he could handle the improved level of pitching.

"He hit the ball harder and more often than anyone I had ever seen," said former Cannons' teammate Bo Hart. "Even when he made an out, it was simply because he had happened to hit a line drive right at a fielder, not because the pitcher had overpowered him."

The word about Pujols had spread throughout the Cardinals organization, so when Gaylen Pitts, who was the manager of their Triple-A Memphis (Tennessee) Redbirds, needed an extra right-handed hitter, he asked the organization's front office to send him the kid who had been making so much noise with his bat.

"They were a little reluctant at first," recalled Pitts. "I understood their concern. He had only been in professional baseball for a few months, and the move from Class-A to Triple-A in a single season is a big jump. I mean, the year before he was playing in junior college and I'm asking them to put him on a hot seat, at the highest level of minor league play. I know that they were afraid that he might be overmatched and get discouraged and go into a shell. It wouldn't be the first time that a young player had been ruined by bringing him along too quickly."

What's more, the Redbirds were only a few days away from the start of the Pacific Coast League playoffs, a situation that was bound to put pressure on a young player. Pitts was also asking for Pujols to play left field, a position that he had never played before. The organization also knew that it was very unusual for any first-year professional, even a top draft choice, let alone a 13th round draft choice, to ride all the way up from the lowest to the highest level of the minors. It was finally decided to let him play in the team's final few regular season games. If he held his own, he'd be put on the Memphis roster for the playoffs, and if he looked overmatched, he'd ride the bench and wait for the Arizona Fall League season to start.

But Pujols passed his brief regular-season test with flying colors, then went on to hit for a .302 overall average in the playoffs. But he was at his best when it counted most, as he hit .367 and led the Redbirds to the Pacific Coast league championship when he ripped a game-winning home run in the 13th inning of the final game in the series. His late-inning heroics also clinched the series MVP award for Pujols, who had hit a pair of homers and driven in five runs in the seven game series.

"Albert showed that he was the kind of kid who didn't have to be treated with kid gloves," said Pitts. "Just put a bat in his hands and let him take his cuts, he'll hold his own against anybody."

Then, Pujols topped off his amazing climb through the Cardinals' farm system by hitting .323 and rapping 21 RBI in just 27 games in the Arizona Fall League. The circuits' coaches and managers were impressed and voted him the league's third-best prospect.

"He was a kind of one-man wrecking crew," noted Mike Jorgensen. "At that point, it was obvious to me that he was going to be a special kind of player, and not just a top-notch hitter."

5   A DREAM COME TRUE

During the winter, Pujols worked in the catering department of a local country club, and he and Deidre and Isabella moved in with his in-laws, so that the couple could save money on rent. The extra money became even more necessary in January, when Deidre gave birth to a son, Alberto, Junior, who was quickly nicknamed A.J.

It was during this time that Pujols received the news that the Cardinals had decided to invite him to work out with the big league team at their spring training base in Jupiter, Florida. The invitation was about rewarding him for his achievements the year before, and giving him a small taste of what life in the big leagues is like. It's also possible that the front office wanted to show Pujols what the level of play at the major league level is all about; wanted him to realize that as fast as he had risen up the minor league ladder, that the next step, if he could eventually take it, would be, by far, the biggest one. From that perspective, the invitation was supposed to serve as a reality check, to point out to Pujols the gap between where he was at and where he needed to get to.

When Pujols shared the news with Marty Kilgore, his former junior college coach spoke about how much fun it would be in infield drills to throw baseballs across the diamond to the Cardinals' first baseman, Mark McGwire, who had swatted 70 homers in 1998.

"I mean, no one expected Albert to make the jump to the Cardinals after only one season in the minors, it just doesn't happen that way," explained Kilgore. "But Albert just looked at me with a very determined stare and said, 'I am not going there to throw to Mark McGwire. I'm going there to make the team.'"

Between his job and the responsibilities of family life, Pujols still managed to carve out a significant amount of time to work out and to hone his baseball skills. He knew that if he was going to have any chance to go north with the Cardinals, he would have to come to spring training in prime-time shape and get off to a quick start. He realized that the organization wasn't going to invest too many at-bats in a player with only one year of professional ball under his belt—unless that player did things that forced them to pay attention to him.

When Pujols arrived at the Cardinals' spring training site he discovered that he had been assigned No. 68, and he knew that the high number was a sure sign that the Cardinals didn't expect him to be around very long. But he approached his every turn in the batting cage with focus and purpose, and the coaching staff started to take notice of his ability.

"He was taking really professional at-bats," said Cards' pitching coach Dave Duncan. "You could tell that he was determined to compete from the moment he took his first practice swings. Even though it was only batting practice in February, he treated every at-bat as though it was a game-winning situation in the regular season. He didn't waste any swings, or chase after bad pitches. He had a very disciplined and mature approach to hitting, which really caught my eye."

At that point, however, it seemed as though there wasn't anything that Albert could do to crack the Cards' veteran line-up. He was so far out of their plans, in fact, that Cards' manager Tony La Russa didn't even assign Albert a permanent position and, instead, kept moving him around the diamond, playing him not only at third base, but also at first, shortstop, and in the outfield, as well.

"It was obvious that he had a lot of talent, and I thought that he had a chance to make it to the bigs," said La Russa. "But I didn't think there was any way that he was going to do it without a full year in Triple-A, so I just used him to fill in wherever I needed him."

Pujols, however, had other plans and his hitting and his play in the field started to make La Russa have second thoughts about sending him back to Memphis.

"Playing in the minors was a lot of fun, even the 10-hour bus rides," noted Pujols. "But after a taste of the majors, I didn't want to go back there."

Pujols had also caught the attention of people outside the Cards' organization, including San Francisco Giants manager Felipe Alou, the first Dominican-born manager in major league history.

"I saw a lot of Albert that spring, and it seemed like everything he hit was *hard*," said Alou, whose team at the time, the Montreal Expos, shared the Jupiter training camp complex with St. Louis. "It really surprised me to see a hitter who had been at Class-A the previous year develop so quickly."

Although La Russa had ticketed him for a trip back to Triple-A before he had even arrived in Jupiter, Pujols made the job of cutting him tougher than had been expected by posting a .349 batting average in 62 at-bats, and leading the Cards in total bases. But Pujols still had one foot on the bus back to Memphis when Bobby Bonilla, a Cardinals' outfielder suffered an injury near the end of the Grapefruit League season. The injury opened up a roster spot and La Russa told Pujols that he would start the season with St. Louis, but that he would probably be sent down after the team's first series, when Bonilla was expected back in the line-up.

"I was fortunate enough to get a chance to make the team," noted Pujols. "But that wouldn't have mattered if I didn't believe that I *could* make the team."

Walt Jocketty, who was team's general manager at the time, had come to the conclusion that whether or not Pujols was ready to stay in the big leagues at that time, that he was going to turn out be a special player. So, he decided that Pujols should be given a *significant* number, which to the general manager meant a single-digit number.

"You look at the ones we've retired—Stan Musial, Red Schoendienst, Ozzie Smith—they're single digits," noted Jocketty, speaking of three of the team's Hall of Famers. "It's hard to explain, but I think they look better."

Pujols, playing left field, poked a single for his first major league hit on opening day against the Rockies, in

Colorado. Although it was his only hit during the three game series, Pujols took heart from the fact that he had consistently put good wood on the ball.

"I hit the ball hard, so I didn't get frustrated," he explained. "I knew what I could do."

Then, he showed everybody what he could do in the team's next series, when he hammered the Arizona Diamondbacks pitching staff for seven hits in 14 at-bats. The most notable of those seven hits was a two-strike, two-run double against Arizona's ace, Randy Johnson, who would go on to capture the 2001 National League Cy Young Award, the third in his string of four straight first-place finishes in the Cy Young Award voting.

"When he rocked that double off of Randy Johnson, everyone in the dugout opened their eyes wide," said former teammate Mark McGwire. "Right there, we knew we had a hitter."

Although La Russa had Pujols hitting sixth in the batting order, injuries to McGwire and others caused him to move Pujols up two spots to the clean-up position. It was a move that La Russa had been hesitant to make because he, like other managers, is reluctant to put too much pressure on a rookie, and clean-up hitters are supposed to be a team's biggest run producers.

For the same reason, managers don't like to move players from position to position on the field, which can be distracting and can also cause them to lose concentration at the plate. Injuries, though, caused La Russa to move Pujols around the field, as though he was a pawn on a chessboard. But Pujols responded to the constant changes with total professionalism and without a peep, as he moved from the outfield to the infield, from first base to third base, wherever he was needed.

"I wanted to be in the lineup every day, and playing somewhere is better than sitting on the bench," noted Pujols.

"You see a lot of rookies who look overmatched at this level," said Bob Brenly, who was the Diamondbacks' manager. "Other rookies have a look in their eyes that lets you know they think that they belong. Albert certainly has that look."

Pujols had more than the look, he also had the stick, and he swung it so well that the idea of sending him back down to Memphis was replaced by the realization that he was in the big leagues to stay.

"What he did, right out of the gate, surprised me," said La Russa. "But after watching him handle himself for a few weeks, it didn't take a rocket scientist to realize that Albert was major league ready."

In his first month in the big leagues, Pujols, in fact, was near the top of the NL hitting charts with a .370 average, 27 RBI, in only 24 games, and eight dingers, which tied the major-league record for home runs by a rookie in April.

Pujols continued his assault on big league pitching through the first three months of the 2001 season before he finally suffered through his first slump, a 2-for-33 sag in early July. But he still came into the mid-point of the season among the league leaders in virtually every major hitting category, and was selected to play in the All-Star Game, a rare honor for a first-year player.

When the calendar turned to the dog days of August,

Pujols heated up along with the temperature, as he went on a 17-game hitting streak that helped lead the Cards to within six games of the Central Division lead.

"He's focused in everything he does, from hitting to running down the line," said Hall of Famer Red Schoendienst. "He doesn't just go through the motions."

Heading into September, Pujols was already a lock for the NL Rookie of the Year award, but a number of people started touting him as an MVP contender, including Mark McGwire.

"There's no doubt in my mind that if we make the playoffs, Albert should be an MVP candidate," said Big Mac. "He respects everyone and everything about the game, but this kid isn't in awe of anything or anyone."

St. Louis did, in fact, make it into the 2001 playoff picture, as they closed in a rush in September and managed to finish in a dead-heat with the Houston Astros for the division title with a 93-69 record.

"He's my MVP," said Mark McGwire. "If we didn't have him, I don't know where we would have finished."

The Cards, however, came up a game short in the opening round of the playoffs, losing 3-games-to-2 to the Diamondbacks, who went on to win a classic World Series against the New York Yankees. Pujols, who collected only two hits in 18 at-bats against the D-Backs, didn't do much to help the Cardinals' cause, but nothing that happened in the post-season could diminish his astonishing, record-setting accomplishments in the regular season.

In his first season in the big leagues, Pujols set the National League rookie marks for RBI (130), extra-base hits (88) and total bases (360), and became only the second Cardinal rookie to lead the team in RBI, home runs (37), and average (.329).

"For Albert to do what he did for six months is just phenomenal," said La Russa. "If he had been a 10-year veteran, it still would have been exceptional, but to have done it in his rookie season is just unbelievable. Everything about Albert is legitimate, and he's going to be doing this for a long time."

The Baseball Writers of America agreed, and unanimously selected Pujols as the winner of the Jackie Robinson National League Rookie of the Year Award.

"It's nice to be recognized, and it shows what can be accomplished if you work hard and believe in yourself," said Pujols, who finished fourth in the voting for the MVP Award. "But I don't think about awards and records. I just want to help my team win, and we came up a little bit short this year."

6 A LEGEND IN THE MAKING

While Pujols knew that the long road to the Hall of Fame was filled with players who had captured Rookie of the Year honors, he also knew that the award had gone to some one-shot wonders, who had quickly faded into obscurity. Pujols was determined to prove that his production in 2001 wasn't a fluke, but the start of a great career.

To accomplish his goal and to avoid joining the legion of players who had suffered from the *sophomore slump*, a not uncommon second-year fall-off in production that had snared so many players before him, Pujols quickly put the success of the 2001 season behind him and spent the off-season getting ready for the 2002 season.

"It's not what you did last year that counts," declared Pujols. "It's what you're going to do this year. That's more important. What's more, I don't believe in jinxes. I believe in hard work and preparing myself to play the best that I can, so that I can help my team win."

Instead of resting on his rookie laurels, Pujols spent countless hours during the off-season working out and watching videotape of opposing pitchers, studying their deliveries for weaknesses that he would be able to exploit. He also spent hours watching tape of some of the game's best hitters, seeing what he could learn by watching the way they handled their plate appearances.

"I learn so much by watching great hitters like Todd Helton and Alex Rodriguez," explained Pujols. "They've been successful for a lot longer than I have, so I'd have to be pretty stupid or arrogant to think that I couldn't benefit from watching the way they approach different pitchers and situations."

If he was going to slump in his second season in the big leagues, it wasn't going to happen because of his failure to prepare as well as he could.

"I won't throw this opportunity away," he announced upon his arrival at spring training. "I won't be lazy or take things for granted. I don't want to be cocky and think I'm the best. I want to stay humble and keep working as hard as I can, so I can get as good as I can."

His attitude and work habits were noticed by his teammates and the coaching staff, who were delighted to see that his head hadn't swelled and that he was determined to continue establishing his credentials as a bona fide big league star.

"He works harder now than he did as a rookie," noted Tony La Russa. "And it was his work ethic, more than his talent, which won him the respect of the veterans on this club when he first came to spring training last year."

Another component of his success is his willingness to use his head by listening to and absorbing good advice from respected sources.

"I'm a really smart player," explained Pujols, without a trace of arrogance. "If you tell me something, I get it quickly. If there is something wrong with my hitting, tell me what's wrong and I'll pick it up right away. That's the best thing I have going for me, my ability to listen to a coach and fix what I'm doing wrong."

Mitchell Page, who was the Cardinals' hitting coach at the time, raved about the commitment to excellence that Pujols exhibited in every aspect of his approach to the game.

"He has the best work habits I've ever seen on a young kid," Page had exclaimed. "He takes nothing for granted. But his work doesn't stop when he puts the bat down. He's constantly trying to improve as a fielder, and he's always asking questions, always trying to take it to the next level."

Despite all that effort and preparation, Pujols got off to a slow start in 2002, stymied by the work that opposing pitchers and coaches had done to find holes in his swing. In the constant game of cat and mouse that goes on between pitchers and hitters, the hurlers had managed to get, however temporarily, the upper hand.

To counter the adjustments that had been made against him, Pujols worked every day in the batting cage to close the holes in his swing, and then went into the clubhouse to watch videotape of those plate appearances.

"That's how you become a good hitter," he explained. "You don't want to have three bad at-bats and then try to figure it out. You want to make adjustments after your first at-bat. And even after a good trip to the plate, you want to see what you did right, so that you can repeat the lesson in your next at-bat."

Just when the talk about Pujols succumbing to the sophomore slump heated up, he turned around his season with a sizzling August surge that saw him hit for a

.368 average and drive in 32 runs. Although he had struggled with an unexpectedly low average through July, his confidence had never dipped.

"I wasn't concerned that it took awhile to get my average up above .300," he explained. "I was driving in runs and helping my team win, and that's always the bottom line for me. I worked hard and, like I've always known, if I work hard, good things are going to happen."

His calm demeanor in the face of adversity is one of the backbones of his personality, a quality that allows him to face up to a challenge, instead of allowing it to overwhelm him.

"I don't put pressure on myself," he explained. "I just concentrate on what I need to do, and do it the best I can. I make it a habit to do my best every day, and try to help my team to win any way I can."

His ability to block out pressure in a sport where pitchers are routinely throwing a ball at better than 90-MPH, and 40,000 people are either cheering for him or booing him, depending upon whether he's playing at home or away, has gained him many fans within the game.

"He stands like a man," said Felipe Alou. "They didn't teach him fear where he grew up. It's not part of his bag."

Although his batting average might have started to head north in August regardless of what happened around him, it certainly didn't hurt him any when the Cards pulled off a blockbuster trade with the Philadelphia Phillies on July 29 that brought Scott Rolen to St.

Louis. With Rolen's big bat hitting behind him, pitchers became less likely to nibble at the corners or pitch around Pujols, and more likely to put pitches squarely in the strike zone. The addition of Rolen, a perennial Gold Glove third baseman, also meant that Albert had one less fielder's mitt to keep in his locker and one less position he had to prepare to play.

As much as Pujols appreciated having Rolen batting behind him and making the team stronger offensively as well as defensively, the third baseman quickly came to admire how Pujols played the game.

"You see him twice a year and you figure you're catching him when he's hot," said Rolen. "When you're on the same team, you realize he's like that every day. You think he has to cool off sometimes, but he doesn't. He's that good."

With Pujols, Rolen, and Gold Glove center fielder Jim Edmonds, a left-handed power hitter, supplying the muscle, and closer Jason Isringhausen anchoring the pitching staff, the Cards ran away from their divisional rivals and captured the Central Division crown with a 97-65 record.

The Cards, once again, drew the Diamondbacks in the opening round of post-season play, but this time they trumped Arizona with a three-game sweep of the D-Backs. But that turned out to be the end of the road for St. Louis, whose bid for the NL pennant was sideswiped by the San Francisco Giants, 3-games-to-2, leaving the Cards one win away from playing in the 2002 World Series. The series between the Cards and the Giants had been billed as a battle between San Francisco' perennial superstar, Barry Bonds, who had led the majors with a .370 batting average, and Pujols, St. Louis' bright new nova, but neither player produced the fireworks that both of them were expected to ignite.

Pujols, who had finished his second sensational season with a .314 average (the lowest average in his seven-year career), 34 big flies, 118 runs scored and 127 RBI, finished right behind Bonds in voting for the league MVP Award. In proving that the sophomore slump would not claim him as a victim, Pujols, instead of faltering, built on his spectacular rookie year by becoming the first player in big league history to hit at least .300 with 30 homers, 100 RBI, and 100 runs scored in each of his first two seasons.

"He is the whole package," declared Tony La Russa. "There's going to be a time when we all look back and say, 'Wow, we got to see that man play early in his career, before he became a legend.'"

7 TAKING IT TO THE LIMIT

After spending another off-season working out and spending some quality time with his family, Pujols came to spring training ready to continue taking his game to a higher level. Although he had already put together two seasons that the great majority of players can only dream of achieving even once, Pujols, as always, was looking forward, not backward.

Unlike the previous year, Pujols started the 2003 season with a red-hot bat, as he posted a .385 average in April and then pounded 10 homers and racked up 26 RBI in May.

"I've managed my share of outstanding players, from Ricky Henderson to Mark McGwire, but Albert is the best of all," said Tony La Russa. "I know that it's only the start of his third season, but I've already seen enough."

Pujols continued on his hitting rampage throughout the spring and early summer, as he posted a .429 average with 29 RBI in June, and headed into the halfway point of the season as the hottest hitter in baseball. In a summer of memorable at-bats for Pujols, some people point to a July 4th match-up against Kerry Wood, the Chicago Cubs' right-hander, who throws heat at about 100-MPH, as one of the signature moments.

As the hot summer sun poured down on Chicago's

famed Wrigley Field, Wood put Pujols on his backside with a 98-MPH two-seam fastball that all but shaved some of the hair off of Pujols' chin.

In an age when too many players are too quick to charge the mound and start a fight, Pujols just stood up and stepped back into the batter's box. Then, he crushed Wood's next pitch over the ivy-covered wall, a blast that helped the Cards topple the Cubs.

"You don't rattle him," said Jim Edmonds afterwards, his lips curled into an appreciative smile. "He rattles you."

His great start had captured the attention of fans all around the country and they responded by making Pujols the top vote-getter for the National League All-Star team. Pujols had a great time visiting with the other major league stars, and came in second in the Home Run Derby, behind Garret Anderson of the California Angels.

"I had a couple of guys from the American League who had challenged my statement that Albert was the best player I had ever managed," said La Russa afterwards. "But after the All-Star Game they told me, 'We thought when you made that statement that you were just exaggerating to make a point. But now we understand what you were talking about. He's an *awesome* talent.'"

Of course, talent is only one of the elements that go into making a great player. The world is filled with people who have talent but never make it past their local street corner, because they don't have the discipline to develop it, the perseverance to practice it, or the good sense to stay away from drugs, alcohol and criminal activity.

But no one has ever had to tell Pujols to practice more or stay away from drugs or any other negative behaviors. From high school to the big leagues, he has worn out coaches and batting practice pitchers, doing everything he can to take his talent to the limit.

"I've never seen a young player as disciplined as he is," said Mitchell Page. "He constantly watches video, and everything he does has a purpose, there's no down-time with Albert. You watch him, even in the pre-game drills, and you see how determined he is. He learned a hitting drill from A-Rod, where he hits off a tee, just to make sure that he keeps his stroke level and doesn't develop any bad habits. And the reality of it is, his swing is a thing of beauty. I look at his swing and I think of names like Ted Williams, Rod Carew, and George Brett, guys who had beautiful swings. It's a gift, and that type of gift dosen't come around very often."

Although St. Louis faded from the playoff race in September, done in by a depleted pitching staff, Pujols continued his season-long tear and confirmed his position as one of the top hitters in the game. By the end of the 2003 season, Pujols led all major leaguers in six offensive categories, including average (.359); runs scored (137); doubles (51); extra-base hits (95); and total bases (394). His phenomenal performance, which also included 43 homers, 124 RBI, 212 hits, and only 65 strikeouts, was one of the finest ever compiled by any player in the long and storied history of the St. Louis Cardinals. And at only 23 years of age, Pujols had become the youngest player to win a batting title since Tommy Davis, a former outfielder with the Los Angeles Dodgers had turned the trick in 1962, when he, too, was 23.

But those monster stats weren't enough to earn the MVP Award for Pujols, who was again beaten out by Barry Bonds in voting by the Baseball Writers of America. But Pujols' peers showed their disagreement with that outcome by naming him the winner of the Players' Choice Major League Player of the Year Award, and choosing him as the National League's Outstanding Player.

"I've played with great players, guys who put up some good numbers," said former teammate Tino Martinez. "But I've never seen a guy as focused as he is. He's just amazing."

During his first three years in the majors, Pujols had, in fact, put up numbers which compared favorably with the best career starts that any player had ever posted. His 114 big flies, for example, had tied the record for the most home runs hit in a player's first three seasons, which had been set by Hall of Famer Ralph Kiner. While Pujols was aware of the fact that his career was off to a powerful start, he still remained focused on what lay ahead of him.

"Of course I want to be considered one of the game's best players when I retire from baseball," said Albert, who made only three errors during the 2003 season, while playing 113 games in left field and 36 at first base. "I want to play well enough to make it to the Hall of Fame. But we're a long way from there, and I still have a lot more to accomplish."

8   NO CEILING IN SIGHT

The Cardinals had so much faith in Pujols' future that in February of 2004 they signed him to a franchise-record, seven-year, $100 million contract, the highest amount ever paid to any third-year player. And he was quick to assure people that the large contract wouldn't affect his commitment to excellence.

"I will keep working hard, both mentally and physically, because I know if you feel too comfortable, that's when someone comes from the minor leagues and takes your spot," explained Pujols. "I came out of nowhere and took someone's job, and someone else can come along and do the same to me, if I slack off."

Pujols also felt that he had a responsibility not only to the Cardinals, but also to the immigrant community and to all the fans that were following his career.

"I hope I'm a role model for the millions of people who come to this country with the same dreams that my family had," said Pujols, who had made an amazing journey from childhood poverty and an insecure future. "But I also want to be a role model for everyone, no matter where they were born, or what the color of their skin is. When I walk out of the game, I want to be remembered as one of the best players, but I also want people to remember me as one of the best people; as someone who respected my fans and gave something back to them."

Pujols began to back up his words the following year, when he started a foundation that provides assistance to the families and children who live with Down syndrome and to improve the standard of living of poor children in the Dominican Republic through education, medical relief and needed supplies.

Pujols, who took over as the every day first baseman, quickly showed that he was worth the investment that the Cardinals had made by finishing among the NL leaders in every major offensive category, while leading all major league players in runs, total bases, and extra-base hits.

"He's unbelievable," said Scott Rolen. "He's on it 162 games a year. I've never seen anyone else like him. I'm lucky if I'm on it for 100 games…or for that matter, 62 games."

Although Pujols had produced a fourth straight season of superstar dimensions, he wasn't the only All-Star in the Cardinals clubhouse. Rolen, who set career highs with 34 big flies and 124 RBI, and Jim Edmonds, who matched his career high with 42 home runs, and posted a career-best 111 RBI, were the major thumpers behind Pujols in the batting order, while shortstop Edgar Renteria and second baseman Tony Womack were the table-setters for the wrecking crew that followed them.

The Cardinals also had a fine pitching staff, which was led by starters Chris Carpenter, Jeff Suppan, and Jason Marquis, and anchored by closer Jason Isring-hausen, who had tied for the league lead with 47 saves.

With that array of talent, the Cardinals went out and posted a 105-57 mark, the best record in baseball, and only one win away from the franchise record that had been set in 1942. So, it wasn't surprising that they opened the playoffs as the odds-on favorites to capture the NL pennant, and they took the first step toward that goal by knocking off the Los Angeles Dodgers in four games, as Pujols contributed a pair of homers and five RBI. His first big fly started a Cards' rout in Game 1, and his second, a 3-run shot, was the game-winner in the Game 4 clincher.

But his hitting in the division series was just a warm-up for his heroics in the National League Championship Series against the Astros, when he and Houston center fielder Carlos Beltran combined to put on what might be the greatest hitting display in post-season history.

Beltran, who now plays for the New York Mets, had already set the tone for his heroics by blasting four round trippers and driving in nine runs while leading the Astros past Atlanta in their division series, 3-games-to-2.

The two stars ignited the fireworks in the first pair of games between the Cards and Astros, as Beltran did his part by hitting a home run in each of the two games. But Pujols answered the challenge and thrilled his hometown fans by hitting a two-run shot in the first inning of Game 1, and the game-winning big fly in the eighth inning of Game 2.

"It's amazing to think that he's gotten better every year," said Jason Isringhausen. "And he doesn't seem to have a ceiling."

The Cards high-powered motor stalled out in Houston, however, which allowed the Astros to take the next three games and put the Cards on the edge of elimination. The third loss had been particularly trying for Pujols, who had gone hitless in four at-bats, and had failed to come through when the team had needed him.

"I can't do it every time," said Pujols. "I'm a human being, not a machine. All I can do is try my best. I feel bad that I had an opportunity where I could have put my team on top, but didn't deliver. On the other hand, you have to tip your hat to the other team. Sometimes you just get beat. But tomorrow's a different day, and I'll go out to try my best, again, and we'll see what happens."

Pujols got the Cards off to a quick start in Game 6, when he stroked a two-run homer in the opening inning, and he smacked a double that ignited a two-run rally in his next at-bat. Then, in the 12th inning, he drew a walk and scored the winning run when Jim Edmonds hit a walk-off big fly that kept the Redbirds alive for another day.

The season had come down to a winner take all Game 7, and the Astros dealt their ace Roger Clemens, the only seven-time Cy Young Award-winner in baseball history. With Clemens throwing darts and appearing all but unhittable, the Astros 2-1 lead with two outs in the bottom of the sixth looked a lot larger than the scoreboard indicated, even through the Cards had a runner on third and Pujols at the plate.

Pujols, who had only two hits to show for his 14 career at-bats against Clemens, fell behind in the count at 1-2, as time seemed to slow and the tension in Busch Stadium seemed to rise with each pitch. Clemens' next delivery was a fastball thrown at the inside edge of the plate, a pitch that has helped him strike out thousands of batters. But Pujols was able to turn on the pitch and crack a game-tying RBI double into the left-field corner, a hit that set off a high-decibel roar, which was part elation but mostly relief that the spell that Clemens had been weaving was broken. Just how broken became obvious after Scott Rolen ripped his next pitch over the left wall, which gave the Cardinals a 4-2 lead and all the runs they would need to capture the game and the 2004 National League pennant.

"That last at-bat against Clemens is one of the best I've ever had," said Pujols, as he stood in the locker room afterwards and his teammates celebrated around him. "I'm going to be dreaming about it for the next couple of weeks."

Pujols, who hit .500 against the Astros, with four homers and nine RBI, was named the MVP of the National League Championship Series, and was on his way to the World Series. Whereas Beltran, who had hammered four homers against the Cards, set an LCS record with 12 runs scored, and had been as overall brilliant as Pujols had, just went home.

"Carlos was unbelievable," said Pujols. "I've never seen a player get that hot over so many games. I'm just glad that we were able to survive his outburst and take that last game, because going to the Word Series is what you dream about when you're a little boy. It doesn't get any better than that."

But the Cardinals' exciting ride ran into a roadblock

in the form of the Boston Red Sox, who derailed their dreams with a four-game sweep. The swiftness of Boston's win, its first World Series victory in 86 years, left the Cardinals feeling somewhat dazed.

"I knew they were a tough team, and that we would have our hands full," said Pujols, looking stunned at having his season end so suddenly. "But I didn't think any team could take four straight from us."

9   THE MVP

If any player ever had the right to feel complacent about his accomplishments, Pujols certainly would have been near the top of the list. In his first four seasons, he had compiled numbers that surpassed the first four seasons of virtually all of the all-time greats of the game, and he had also spearheaded the Redbirds drive to the 2004 NL pennant. But he wasn't interested in comparisons, or in being stopped short of his ultimate goal.

"I don't compare myself to other players," said Pujols, who reported to spring training after he'd worked out five days a week during the winter to help him prepare for the 2005 season. "Don't get me wrong, I respect what all the great players have done, but it's not my job to make comparisons. I get paid to help my team win.

"Last year I got a taste of the World Series, but it didn't turn out the way I wanted it to. Hopefully, we'll get another crack at it this year. But the winning doesn't come in a package. You have to work hard to get there, and that's why I made sure I got myself ready for the season. What I lose today, I can't make up tomorrow. I have to do it today. That's what it's all about."

That sense of urgency helped Pujols post a season-long stretch of high-level consistency that saw him hit for better than a .300 average during every month of the season, except for August, when he dipped down to .287, while his on-base percentage was higher than .400 in every month but April, when it slipped to .396.

"We talk about Barry Bonds having been the greatest hitter of our time right now," said Washington Nationals' general manager Jim Bowden. "Get ready for Albert Pujols, because he's next. He's got the potential to be one of the greatest hitters ever to play the game. That's not an exaggeration. That's what he is."

Pujols is also a team leader, who is always ready to lend a helping hand and tutor the younger players.

"I try to pass it along, the same way that veteran players helped me when I came up," he explained. "Hopefully, in five years, they can do the same for somebody else. And it's not just about helping the younger players. Jimmy might tell me I'm holding my hands too low. And if I see something that's out of sync with Scott, I'll tell him. We all pull for each other. That's why we won 105 games last year, and why we've been to the postseason in four of the past five years. Everybody helps each other."

The Cardinals hung together so well that they hit the century mark in wins and posted the best record in baseball for the second straight season. It was an outstanding accomplishment for a team that had lost three key starters—Renteria, Womack and Mike Metheny, their Gold Glove Award-winning catcher—to free agency and that also had to cope with the absence of Scott Rolen, who missed two thirds of the season with an injury. A key element in the Cards' success was its pitching staff, which led the majors with a 3.49 earned run average. At the top of the starting rotation was Chris Carpenter, who went 21-5, and earned the National League Cy Young Award, while Mark Mulder, who had been acquired in a trade, did the job he was brought in to do by notching 16 wins. The relievers also played their part, especially Jason Isringhausen, who notched 39 saves and posted a miniscule 2.14 earned run average.

The Redbirds continued their winning ways with a three-game sweep of the San Diego Padres in the opening round of the 2005 playoffs, which earned them a return trip to the LCS and a return match against the Astros, who made it into the post-season as a wild-card entry after finishing 11 games behind the Cards in the regular season. But after a loss in Game 1, the Astros shocked the Cards by running off three straight wins and taking a 4-2 lead into the top of the ninth inning of Game 5.

The fans in Houston's Minute Maid Park were on their feet and roaring with every pitch as Brad Lidge, one of the league's top closers, retired the first two batters and was one out away from pitching the Astros to the pennant. But after David Eckstein, the Cards' pesky shortstop, singled, Jim Edmonds drew a walk, which brought Pujols into the batter's box.

The noise of the crowd grew to near-deafening, as Lidge got ahead in the count, 0-1, but Pujols, who had been hitless in four trips to the plate, sucked the noise and the life out of Minute Maid by cracking a 412-foot drive over the left field fence that gave the Cards a 5-4 lead and sent the series back to St. Louis.

"It was amazing how quickly the silence fell on the crowd," said Pujols. "It went from being so loud that I couldn't hear the guys in the on-deck circle, to hearing my own footsteps as I rounded the bases. That's never happened to me before. Hopefully, I'll get more big hits in this series, and then some more in the World Series."

But those hopes were snuffed in the following game, as Houston took Game 6, and Pujols was forced to strand aside and watch the Astros celebrate the first pennant in the team's forty-four year existence.

Although Pujols had failed to reach his ultimate team goal, he did, finally, win the National League MVP Award, after posting another sensational season, during which he amassed a .330 average, 41 homers and 117 RBI. The voting for the award was tight because Andruw Jones, Atlanta's Gold Glove-winning center fielder, and Derrek Lee, the Chicago Cubs' Gold Glove-winning first baseman, had produced career years at the plate, with Jones pacing the league in home runs and RBI, and Lee winning the batting title and topping the charts in many other offensive categories. Although any of the three would have been worthy winners, what stood out was the fact that while the other two needed to have career years just to be considered for the award, Pujols had won it by having a merely typical year.

"That's the amazing thing: 2005 was Albert's *average* season," said Lee, who was gracious about his third-place finish behind Jones. "This is nothing new for him. Not only does he have the talent, but his consistency is also a testament to his character and his work ethic. He has stayed hungry every single season. And what is he? Twenty-five? Whew! He'll be one of the greatest hitters ever before he's through. He's going to be in the Hall of Fame, simple as that."

10   ALL THE WAY

The day after the Redbirds were eliminated from the 2005 playoffs, Pujols called his friend and personal trainer, Chris Mihlfeld, and told him that they needed to get started on his off-season routine, with a special concentration on situational hitting. This from a player who had driven in more go-ahead and game-winning runs than anyone else in the previous two seasons.

"But that's what Albert is all about," said Mihlfeld. "He's always going to find a reason to be unhappy with his game, because he believes if he doesn't do that, his game will level off. He doesn't want to level off."

Pujols' fear of leveling off was almost amusing when one realizes that he had become the first player ever to hit for at least a .300 average, hack more than 30 homers, and rack up more than 100 RBI in each of his first five seasons. Although his level was, for most players, an unreachable ceiling, he was determined to continue working as hard as he could so that he could continue to improve and continue to raise his game to an even higher level.

"Who really cares about what I did in the past five years?" asked Pujols, who did take time off to enjoy the birth of Sophia, his third child. "That's over with. I'm too young to sit back and think about my past accomplishments. All I want to do is win championships."

Although Pujols wasn't interested in his past accomplishments, his manager was mightily impressed.

"When you're taking about the best five-year start in major league history, that's *huge*," said Tony La Russa. "It's historic, and you don't see history made that often. But the best thing about him is that he isn't interested in piling up empty numbers or seeing himself on the highlight shows. He's always trying to do whatever it takes to win the game. I've seen him start off 0-4, but late in the game, if we need a base runner, he'll take a walk to start a rally. And that's what I admire most: He plays the game for the team, not to build up his personal stats."

While Pujols isn't oblivious to his personal achievements, he seems genuine about placing winning at the forefront of his mind. But Cards' hitting coach Hal McRae thinks that his star pupil has some grand personal ambitions that he simply isn't willing to share with other people.

"Everyone else can sit back and marvel at what he's already accomplished, but that isn't what he's about," said McRae, a former All-Star outfielder and manager. "Albert has a fire inside of him that always burns hot. He has some goals that he doesn't talk about. Whatever they are, he's still moving toward them."

Pujols began the 2006 season as though he was, without a doubt, going to reach whatever secret goals he may have set for himself, regardless of how impossibly high he might have set the targets. He got off to a flying start by hitting the first home run in the Cardinals' debut game at the new Busch Stadium, but that was merely the first blast in a month-long barrage that saw him hammer

14 home runs in April, which broke the major league record of 13 that had been held by Ken Griffey, Jr, and Luis Gonzalez.

"He's as gifted a hitter as I've seen come along in a very long time," said Hall of Fame manager Sparky Anderson. "Before he's done, we might be saying he's the best of them all."

By the first week of June, Pujols had already amassed 25 home runs and 65 RBI, and was on track to break the all-time single-season home run record of 73 that had been set by Barry Bonds in 2001.

"There is no ceiling for this guy," said David Ortiz, the Boston Red Sox' big bopper. "I guarantee you he's going to have a career year. I wouldn't be surprised if he hits 60 or more home runs this year."

But just as Pujols' numbers seemed headed for the stratosphere, he suffered an injury that put him on the sideline for 15 games and hopelessly sidetracked his run at the record book. But one day after his return to the lineup, Pujols was back rocking the ball, and he finished the season with career highs in home runs (49) and RBI (137), and was the only player in the National League to finish among the top five in batting average, homers, RBI, runs, on-base percentage, slugging percentage and batting average with runners in scoring position.

"There are some hitters who rate a '10' in *some* categories," said La Russa. "But Albert is a 10 in *all* the important categories."

As usual, Pujols was at his best when the team needed him the most. In a season in which the Cardinals needed every win they could scratch out, just to make it into the playoffs, Pujols hit 20 game-winning home runs, which represented nearly a quarter of the team's total of 83 victories. But none were bigger than the two game-winning clouts he hit in the final week of the season, which helped lift the slumping Redbirds to their third straight division title.

"Those were the hugest of the huge," said La Russa, speaking of the two game-winning big flies that had rescued the Cardinals' season. "Albert is the greatest prime-time hitter in baseball, and he proved it again, right when we needed it the most."

Pujols continued to propel the Cardinals in the opening round of the playoffs, as he drove in the game-winning runs in two of the Cardinals' three wins, providing the production that they needed to defeat the San Diego Padres, 3-games-to-1.

"There's no doubt about it, he's a game-changer," acknowledged Padres outfielder Brian Giles afterwards. "He's a threat every time he's up."

The joy that Pujols felt in advancing deeper into the playoffs was suddenly tempered, however, when he learned of the death of his uncle Antonio, the person who had bought him his first baseball equipment and who had provided him with a childhood home.

"I can't believe he's not here," said Pujols, his cheeks streaked with tears. "I close my eyes and I can still see his face. I still think of him as being alive."

In addition to dealing with his heavy heart, Pujols was also hobbled by a strained hamstring muscle, which severely limited his ability to generate power when he swung his bat. Despite those handicaps, Pujols still managed to hit .317 and help the Cardinals win an exciting seven game series against the New York Mets, who had tied for the best record in baseball with 97 wins. The outcome of the series stayed in doubt until the ninth inning of Game 7, when Cardinals' catcher Yadier Molina hit a go-ahead homer in the top of the ninth at Shea Stadium and then caught the final strike of the game with two out in the bottom of the inning, when rookie pitcher Adam Wainwright froze Carlos Beltran with a knee-breaking strike-three curve ball.

"Nobody gave us a chance, nobody believed in us," noted Pujols, as he celebrated the Cardinals' dramatic pennant-clinching win in the visitors' locker room. "But we never stopped believing in ourselves, and that's why we're going to the World Series."

The Redbirds, whose 83-win season was the second-lowest total ever for a pennant-winning team, were a decided underdog against the American League Champion Detroit Tigers, who had tied the Mets and the New York Yankees for the most wins in the regular season, with 97. But the Cards turned the tables on the Tigers and confounded the so-called experts by taking four out of five games and capturing their first World Series since 1987. Although he wasn't a major factor in the Redbirds' win, no one celebrated more joyously than Pujols, who had achieved his most important goal.

"This is what I've dreamed about, ever since I was a little boy in Santo Domingo," said Albert, a smile spread wide across his face. "I finally have a World Series ring, and that's what I play for. I'm going to enjoy this feeling for a few months, and then I'll be ready to go after the next one."

A few weeks after the World Series had ended, it was revealed that Philadelphia Phillies' first baseman Ryan Howard, who had led the majors in home runs and RBI, had edged Pujols for the National League MVP Award.

"Despite the voting results, Albert is the best player in baseball," declared Tony La Russa. "And before he's finished, he'll be recognized as one of the greatest ever to play the game."

While La Russa might be correct about both of his contentions, and even though his support of one of his players is understandable, his attempt to undermine Howard's achievement was unnecessary.

The announcement also interrupted the sense of bliss that Pujols had been feeling about earning a World Series ring, and he, regrettably, went public with his belief that *he* should have won the award.

"I see it this way: Someone who doesn't take his team to the playoffs doesn't deserve to win the MVP," said Pujols.

It was true that Pujols had been the only hitter in the league to finish in the top five in average, homers, RBI, runs, on-base percentage, and slugging percentage, and he had also won his first Gold Glove Award. So, he could certainly make a legitimate claim for the award on his own behalf. And while it was true that the Phillies didn't make it into the playoffs, they actually won two more games than the Cardinals did. But however one views the criteria for the award—and there are arguments about the subject nearly every year—Howard, a St. Louis native who trains with Pujols in the off-season, was a thoroughly deserving choice, and it was ungracious of Pujols to suggest otherwise.

Howard, in only his second season in the majors, handled the situation in a first-class manner.

"Albert is a great role model," said Howard, who always seems to have a smile on his face. "I'd like to take it to his level and stay up there with him."

After thinking about his own response for a while, Pujols realized that he had been out of line and apologized for his outburst.

"Ryan is a great player and I didn't mean to say anything to suggest otherwise," said Pujols. "I never meant to hurt or disrespect him."

11 WORKING TO BE THE BEST

The Cardinals' successful run to the 2006 World Series title had been an improbable joyride, but the 2007 season would turn out to be anything but joyous. Even before the last of drop of champagne had been sipped in their clubhouse, it was obvious that the coming year was going to be a challenging one for the team.

The afterglow of their triumph couldn't disguise the fact that the Redbirds hadn't been the top team in the National League in 2006, let alone the best overall team in baseball. They had, quite simply, been the team that had managed to get hot at the best possible time, and the front office knew that any hope of having them repeat their magical ride, or even challenge for a playoff spot in 2007, would depend upon their ability to bring in reinforcements through trades and/or free agent signings during the off-season. But instead of strengthening the weak spots on the roster, the Cardinals' saw their already dim prospects get decimated by free agent departures and injuries.

Pujols, meanwhile, was spending his off-season as productively as he ever had, although he did take time off to become a citizen of the USA, passing the test with a perfect score. If anyone thought producing six straight seasons of unequaled excellence or winning a World Series would dampen the fires that drive Pujols, they just hadn't been paying attention. His commitment to his off-season workout remained as relentless as it had always been, and the results even caught the eye of the editors of *Muscle and Fitness* magazine.

"Albert is the poster boy for the evolution of weight training in pro sports," said the magazine's senior editor, Eric Velazquez, who featured Pujols on the May 2007 issue of *Muscle and Fitness*. "His workout routine is even more intense than we had anticipated."

Pujols, however, is careful to use weights to strengthen his body for baseball, and not as a means to bulk up, which would rob him of the flexibility that he needs at the plate and in the field.

"You have to train the right way," explained Pujols, who has been working with a personal trainer since 1999. "But you need to go after it, because it's not going to come after you."

Despite his superb preparation, Pujols got off to a surprisingly slow start in 2007. Usually a torrid early hitter, who starts pounding the ball in spring training, Pujols struggled with his mechanics in the Grapefruit League games.

"Obviously, the last couple of weeks have been tough," he acknowledged a few days before the start of the regular season. "I haven't been seeing the ball too well, and this is the time to do it, because you don't want to have to go into the season worrying about your swing not being right. You want to feel comfortable."

But his struggles at the plate continued into the first month of the season, as he hit the first substantial speed-bump in his seven-year career and finished April with a very un-Pujols like .250 average, and only six home runs, 15 RBI.

"He's been off a little," acknowledged La Russa. "But just remember that old line, 'If *he's* our problem, we don't have a problem.'"

La Russa proved to be right, as Prince Albert recovered from his early-season hitting woes, and by the end of June he had lifted his average to its accustomed place above .300. But the team had problems that couldn't be shrugged off with a quip and, despite the turnaround by Pujols, the Cardinals limped into July 10 games behind the first place Milwaukee Brewers, and fighting a losing battle to reach the .500 mark.

The Cardinals finally did make one surge in the second half of the season, as they went 17-8 from mid-August through early September, to close within a game of the division lead.

"We're actually playing like a team that has a chance," said La Russa, excited by the possibility of capturing lightning in a bottle, the way they had in 2006. "As long as we keep winning, anything can happen."

The Redbirds' move upward in the standings had been fueled by the steady starting pitching of Adam Wainwright and Branden Looper, and the explosive hitting of outfielder Rick Ankiel, who had been called up from Triple-A in early August, and Prince Albert, who hammered home runs in five consecutive games. The last of those big flies was his 30th of the season, making him the first player ever to go deep 30 times in each of his first seven seasons in the majors.

"I think, since his rookie year, he's had us scratching

our heads in amazement at the quality of his baseball, and not just his hitting," said La Russa. "You watch how he plays defense and runs the bases. One way to measure how great a player is in our game is to compare his numbers with those already in the record books, and his numbers speak for themselves. The consistency that he's shown speaks to his strength of mind and competitiveness, even more than just his raw talent."

Although Pujols hit .386 in September, despite playing with a power-depleting leg strain, the Cardinals didn't have enough horses to stay in the race, and they finished the season seven games behind the first place Chicago Cubs in the mediocre Central Division, and six games below .500 at 78-84.

"There are no limits to what he's capable of," said Jim Edmonds. "He just keeps going out there and doing his job. He's always into the game and doing things to help us win. He played hurt, but it didn't seem to take all that much away from his game. He's really fun to watch, and when he's done playing, we'll be talking about how special he was."

Despite playing hurt for a big slice of the season, Pujols still managed to hit for a .327 average, hammer 32 homers and drive in 103 runs, which allowed him to become the only player to collect 30 home runs and 100 RBI in each of his first seven seasons. Although Pujols was pleased to keep his streak intact, his pleasure was diminished by the team's poor showing.

"I've been proud of my numbers in the past because of our great teams," said Pujols. "What does 100 RBI mean if we can't even win 80 games? I don't play for numbers. It's not about numbers. It's all about winning and playing the game the right way. Move a guy over. Steal a base. Make some plays. I play to accomplish certain goals and my top two goals, every year, are to get in the playoffs and win the World Series. I'd gladly trade my streak to be in the post-season and still playing baseball in October."

Although he will have other seasons to reach his lofty goals, the rest of us should just sit back and appreciate the opportunity to watch Pujols, who is just entering his prime years, continue his drive to have his name inscribed among the game's immortals.

"It's pretty simple, really," said Walt Jocketty. "He wants to win and he wants to be the best player of all-time. And he's willing to put in the work to achieve those goals."